To d

Kendi

Love

Jace

THE REFOUNDING OF AMERICA

Launching Lessons for the 21st Century and Beyond

St Germain
Joel D. Anastasi
Phillip Elton Collins

The Angel News Network

This endeavor is dedicated to the higher realms

Beyond the human mind

Ever ready to assist us in our evolution.

Are we ready to once again receive them?

CONTENTS

ISBN: 978-1-54395-744-0

A MESSAGE FROM ST GERMAIN

Beloved students and friends,

It is my great joy and privilege to contribute my newest messages of love and empowerment through the creation of this transformative *Refounding of America, Launching Lessons for the 21st Century and Beyond.*

I have offered many teachings in the past; however, this latest endeavor is one of my most concise, easily accessible and complete teachings told with the support and love of two human proxies for the benefit of humanity.

The purpose of this divine endeavor is to refocus the attention of mankind on the creation and mission of the United States of America as a beacon of light for the entire world.

In Parts 1 and 2 you will be introduced to my two chosen partners in this mission and their adventures leading to our coming together. You also will learn how to apply my higher frequency lessons into your daily lives, nation and world.

Part 3 explains who I am and contains my original transmission of teachings and terms for you to use in making new choices in your lives. You will discover all the necessary tools for the rediscovery of yourselves and for the re-founding of a nation that reflects **your planet's purpose: to create communities of love, equality, harmony and balance.**

Like you, I have had many lifetimes on this planet prior to my ascension into a higher frequency of existence, which is also your destiny. I have been Joseph, the father of Jesus, Merlin, the alchemist at the court of King Arthur, Christopher Columbus, whose status is shifting in your world at present, Francis Bacon, better known as Shakespeare, and, most recently, as Le Comte de Saint Germain in the 18th and 19th century courts of Europe.

I humbly present this divine endeavor for your consideration through your resonance and discernment. I am St Germain, your teacher if you will have me, and friend. I have come to awaken your soul and connect you with the path where your nation will be re-found, and we shall meet.

Imagine what will happen in your lives, nation and world when you choose to become fully conscious, applying the higher realm perspective and wisdom in making new life choices.

Your Teacher & Friend,

St Germain via channel Phillip Elton Collins with co-author Joel D. Anastasi

ABOUT AMERICA

All nations are divine expressions
Of creation's diversified revelations.

But America, for most of her people,
Is much more than they ever dreamed, it seems.

America is an expression of
Divine inclusiveness of mankind
To aspire to reflect ALL THERE IS,
In like kind.

Remember the Founding Fathers' inspirations
Through their founding papers,
Those were never fully fathomed.

America is the heart chakra
And center
Of the spiritual aspirations,
Of Mother Earth, not excluding all her nations.

Through America's creation,
As a nation,
The firm foundation of the
Cosmic Christ Consciousness,
The three sees (3Cs),
Will land in mankind's hearts
And become be's.

No matter how things seem now,
In our social and political nature,
This Mighty Light is in the process
Of growing and expanding throughout Earth's purpose.

Fasten your seat belts.
Many wondrous things
Will be taking place
As the old paradigm melts.

Miracles are not a thing of the ancient past
But very present in the now, at last.

We are entering
The age of Miracles, again,
Revealing the glories
Of the magic stories of the old,
New again.

For America is the consciousness
For this planet.
Reflecting the planetary soul plan, in effect,
Planted in the cosmic concept of consciousness,
That is here, at long last.

THE REFOUNDING OF AMERICA

PART I

Joel D. Anastasi

INTRODUCTION

———

Long, long ago, far, far away—and yet ever so near and pres-ent—the forces of creation set the intention to create a world based upon love, the building block of all there is.

This new world would become a divine experiment that would require the participation of twelve-star systems (where most worlds needed only one) to bring their best qualities into fruition.

This new world, called Earth, would be a direct reflection of cre-ation itself. This reflection is still coming into focus today through a nation designed to have a government of the people, by the people and for the people.

This is the story of that divine experiment told through the lives of three "proxies" serving creation through a nation called The United States of America. Two of the proxies are human; the third became an Ascended Master. All three, however, aspire to the same mission: that the United States and the entire world become full expressions of love, peace, equality, harmony and balance—in essence, reflec-tions of creation itself.

But in the year 2017 it seemed the darkest of times. A dark force had descended over the land of these not so United States of America seeming to destroy the democratic foundations on which the nation was built. Many fell into fear and hopelessness. The divine human experiment of democracy was being tested in an ugly open forum through the malignant wounds and ego defenses of humanity itself.

Yet, there were hopeful signs as well. Suddenly, the same energetic forces that had assisted in creating the nation once again appeared and began to integrate that original founding energy into the people. All that needed to be healed was coming to the surface. This would be another great test in the history of a nation that promised love, equality, harmony and balance to itself and the world.

To transmute the dark forces and restore the original mission would require a grand awakening of the people. The people were mastering the wisdom they needed to learn the way they needed to learn it: Democracy is not a spectator sport. It requires the participation of each and every citizen. Democracy and creation itself are incomplete without you. Each and every person matters; otherwise, you would not be here.

This true narrative will be unbelievable for some and a refreshing reminder to others. So whether you believe the Source of this story or not, sit back and get ready to absorb some truths that will challenge and support what you know about yourself, the creation of the United States of America and even creation itself.

The three protagonists in this story create a proud, towering pyramid whose foundation is formed by two earthly men with diverse, yet, very earthly backgrounds. And at the apex of this pyramid, way-showing the way, an extraordinary being who was once human but is now an ascended master. They all share two things in common that join them in this endeavor: the love of freedom—and a good story.

This true tale tells how the three protagonists are choosing to reset humanity's "soul plan compass" for creating the life you say you want. For human beings have unbalanced their lives and are searching for a way back to their true essence.

The two souls who are assisting Ascended Master St Germain in bringing this Re-founding of America story out into the world were born far apart at the northern and southern boundaries of the eastern United States. One adjacent to the southern home of those hidden forces who have attempted to control humanity for eons and the other on the northern perimeter of the nation near a giant, wondrous waterfall where immigrants from all over the world helped build a mighty nation.

The soul plans, their reason to be here, of these two assisting souls would be reunited during their youthful adulthood in New York City, symbolized by the Statue of Liberty, where their ancient mission of bringing truth into the world would once again ignite. Let the adventure begin.

St Germain

CHAPTER 1:
BEGINNINGS

————————

The introduction to this book, as you can see, was written by St. Germain. His eloquence reflects his earlier incarnation as William Shakespeare, and, quite honestly, I am feeling somewhat intimated. Not just because he writes so beautifully, and I am to pick up where he leaves off, but also because of the writing assignment St Germain has given me.

This is to be a story about a divine experiment called planet Earth, which is still unfolding through a nation called the United States. This story is to be told through the lives of three proxies, two humans and one ascended master. I, Joel Anastasi, am one of the humans. My job is to craft these somewhat disparate pieces into an "adventure story."

It's my own fault. I asked for it. Last year, 2016, I discovered and devoured a green moss colored book, *The "I AM" Discourses,* which presents thirty-three discourses by St Germain dictated to Godfre Ray King, mostly in 1932. The teachings are about the I Am Presence, which is our connection to our eternal God spirit, and how to engage with that divine power to enrich our lives and world.

They are among the most powerful and empowering teachings I have ever encountered. The last discourse is dated January 1, 1935.

Because my birthday is October 2, 1935, I decided that was the date I was conceived and intuited some great significance in that.

The I Am teachings are more than eighty years old (so am I), and much has happened since concerning humanity's spiritual growth and evolution, (See my books, *The Second Coming* and *The Ascension Handbook*). I began asking St Germain, in nightly prayer, to let me bring his teachings up to date, so to speak, to our time.

In October 2016, a small group of us were celebrating a friend's birthday in my apartment when Phillip Collins, the other human proxy in this story, announced St Germain wanted to deliver a message. With Phillip as channel, St Germain said, if we so choose, we would begin an endeavor together in the near future.

In a later conversation, St Germain cautioned, "Beloved student, watch what you ask for."

In preparation for our endeavor, which was to begin in January 2017, St Germain dictated a 103-page book to Phillip comprised of seven discourses containing wisdom about mankind's ascension process and a glossary defining over 600 spiritual terms and tools (Part III of this book.) These teachings were to be the basis of my weekly private discussions with him and occasional public forums Phillip and I conducted in a program we called Divine Discussions. St Germain said I was to write an "adventure story" about my spiritual awakening and to weave these teachings (and others yet to be given) through it.

"Your challenge, beloved student, is for you to see your life as an adventure story."

Yes, dear St Germain. A greater challenge (from my perspective) is to weave your teachings through the story and still keep it an "adventure."

During an automatic writing session, my beloved (spiritual) father Adama (more about him later) communicated: "You are telling the adventure story of your life as an awakening to your divinity. Hold that thought before you, and let it guide you."

Yes, as I look at my life I can see it has been a long, slow process of awakening to my divinity—an awakening I have been incredibly unaware of it and only recently have begun to think of in that way.

Clearly, St Germain is talking about a much greater awakening than just my own. He says, above, it will require a "grand awakening of the people" to transmute the dark forces and restore the original mission of the United States.

I can't think of a more powerful idea to give a giant kick start to that awakening than this magnificent truth: *the forces of creation designed the United States to be the prototype for a world based upon love.*

So this awakening story is about the connection between Creation, planet Earth, the United States and humanity—which, as you have been told, will be represented by two humans, Phillip Collins and me, and an Ascended Master, St Germain, as proxies for humanity.

I'll begin with my story, which, in truth, doesn't feel very divine—at least to me.

CHAPTER 2:
JOEL'S STORY

Who am I? Why am I here? What should I be doing with my life? I seemed to be asking those questions all my life. Maybe everyone does. It was 1976. I had moved from Buffalo to New York City eighteen years before, college degree in hand looking to create a new life, a career and find meaning.

Since moving to New York in 1958, I had completed a second active duty tour in the U.S. Army Reserves (I was recalled for a second tour during the Berlin Crisis n 1961), acquired a master's degree in journalism from Columbia, wrote for a newspaper and a magazine and, through a series of false starts and twists and turns, worked my way into a vice presidency of a major financial services firm (lots of vice presidents.) I was miserable.

My division was being sold; my boss had been fired; promoting financial services meant little to me. I wanted out. To do what? Go where? How could I find meaning? I found my way to a Life/Work Planning class at City College of New York where I hoped to find some answers. Lousy class, but I met a skinny guy ten years younger than I named Phillip Collins who was asking the same questions of life. And I learned how *not* to design a life work planning program—a great lesson when a few years later I created my own.

Fast forward nearly twenty years. Saturday, Labor Day weekend 1995, the seventh anniversary of my partner's death. The day before I had closed on the sale of our country home. The management consulting firm I had worked with, which had given me wonderful opportunities to design and present management workshops around the world, had been sold. Career doors were closing, so I decided to retire. I was spending the holiday weekend alone at my beach rental. Another chapter in my life seemed over. I was lonely—and miserable.

Joel? I was sitting near the water's edge on the beach talking to an acquaintance when I heard my name. It was Phillip Collins walking with a knapsack on his back. I learned later his partner of nearly 30 years had just walked out on him when he heard a voice telling him to walk down the beach. Earlier that day, in a secluded area of dunes, I tearfully had begged God to bring some meaning and companionship into my life.

Phillip was starting his first vacation in years at his beach house. After dinner there one evening, we both shared our love for Jesus and our hunger for spiritual truth. That simple sharing was the beginning of a spiritual journey together which, tiny step by tiny step, has led to wondrous relationships with archangels, ascended masters and a host of higher realm beings—and to this book.

Phillip was no longer the sweet, skinny kid I had met twenty years earlier. He was the high-powered director of marketing for Industrial Light and Magic (ILM), the visual effects division of Lucas Films of Star Wars fame. Phillip was ILM's marketing connection to the international advertising industry, and he never stopped talking—on his cell phone. Cell phones were new (at least to me) in the mid 1990's, and no matter where we were he seemed to be endlessly speaking into one in a bewildering variety of languages to people around the globe.

During one four-hour drive from Ft. Lauderdale to Key West, he spoke constantly to people on several continents but rarely to me. On another trip, high on a rocky outcrop overlooking miles of wilderness in Northern New Mexico, his cell phone shattered the peaceful stillness. Our guide, who apparently had never seen a cell phone, was speechless. A phone ringing on a mountain top? Despite his worldly success, clearly, spirit, not business, drove Phillip.

We shared spirit's attraction. I've always had a longing for God. I can't explain it. It was always there. I was a good little Catholic boy who dutifully went to church every Sunday with my family when at home or with Mama, my grandmother, when I stayed with her in Lockport, NY many summers. We had a string of pictures of me at Holy Communion and Confirmation, rosary in hand. Confession, communion, kneeling before all those statues, a good little boy always trying to do the right thing.

But as a grew older I became increasingly horrified that something was terribly wrong—with me. I liked girls very much as friends—too much, one uncle scolded—because I seemed to enjoy the company of girls more than boys. I soon learned that it wasn't just friendship boys wanted from girls. But I didn't feel the physical attraction they claimed, nor was I attracted to the competitive sports that were the rite of passage for teenage boys. No one noticed that more than my macho Italian father.

I tried to fake it, pretend. I joined the high school sports club when I really preferred the movie club, tried out for football, hated it and dropped out. Loathed baseball and did everything I could to avoid neighborhood games. My mother, who encouraged my intellectual interests but used me as an outlet for her unhappiness, seemed embarrassed. My father ignored me or made demeaning comments and incessantly praised my more athletic cousins.

I couldn't lie to myself any more. I was the abomination my church condemned. Rosaries didn't help. Did God hate me? The shame burned deep in my heart. Increasingly confused and lonely, I developed a stammer so bad I could hardly speak in class. Eyeglasses completed the picture of the hapless nerd.

I was desperate to make friends but had no idea how. Hoping for tips, I went to a Betty Grable movie, "How to be Very Very Popular," (Answer: pretty legs help.) I excelled in school, but my father could care less. My father, my father, my father. Dad, couldn't you find something about me to love or maybe just like? Couldn't anyone? Couldn't I?

Toxic shame. It was years before I learned how profoundly wounding shame can be and how it can sabotage a child's attempt to create a joyful, authentic, fulfilling life. Shame is fertile ground for feelings of unworthiness, not good enough and despair. A great place to begin a spiritual journey?

But where could a young gay man find a spiritual path in the 1950's? Could he today? Creating a healthy life begins with a healthy relationship with self, self-esteem, self-love. My church and my culture taught me to hate who I was. Everyone hated "queers." I had to hide my dark secret—from my family, my teachers, my school mates, everyone. I masked my fear with a smile. Fear hurts. The ache radiated from the forbidden secret buried deep in my heart.

Where could I be free to be me and explore life's possibilities? Not Buffalo.

(OK. I can't resist borrowing that hokey line from the musical, A Chorus Line: "Committing suicide in Buffalo is redundant." Now I often return summers to visit family, enjoy delicious food, beautiful lakes and parks and the great summer weather.)

I knew I had to escape. After graduating from Syracuse University with an economics degree in 1957, I completed six months basic training with the U.S. Army reserves in Ft. Dix, New Jersey. On a weekend visit to nearby New York City, I discovered my future home. After my discharge, I returned home for Thanksgiving weekend. Early Monday morning I embarked on a train (suitcase tied with a rope) bound for my new life in New York City.

I planned to stay with two fraternity brothers until I got a job. Otherwise, I had no idea what I was going to do. I only knew I had to create a new life in New York. I had no contacts, money or plans. I had me. But who was I?

By the time I re-met Phillip on the beach some 37 years later, I still could not answer that question, although, in many ways, I had thrived in New York. I had thoroughly explored its rich cultural life. I made peace with my sexuality, had many friends and a happy relationship with a loving partner. I enjoyed some success as an economics writer, then as an officer in a major financial firm and finally as a management consultant, where I designed and presented management development programs for organizations in the United States and Europe.

But by 1995 much of my life had unraveled. AIDs had ravaged the gay community for more than a decade. It killed my beloved partner, Adam, and many of my friends. My career seemed over. My country house felt empty and lonely. At least the beach offered a chance for human contact and the opportunity to make new friends.

Phillip's call to me on that beach was a lifeline, though I didn't know it was connected to eternity. I'm still discovering what that means. That's where this "re-founding" story really begins, at least for me. For the re-founding of America is, in many ways, a metaphor for the re-founding or the rebirth of self—self, which, St Germain teaches, is a reflection of all that is.

Phillip is one of those high energy, verbal whizzes who can swim with sharks, as they say. If I could use one word to describe him, it would be fearless. His job was to land big budget commercials for his film studio. In the 1980's television screens began to light up with ILM's dazzling commercials sporting the latest visual effects originally created for big budget action films, including the Star Wars sagas. Many ILM ads were featured in high profile Super Bowl and Academy Awards broadcasts.

The world of television commercials looks glamourous, but inflated budgets usually come with oversize egos, and Phillip has ego stories to spare—with clients, directors, stars, etc. He was eager to escape that high pressure, synthetic world, as we both were drawn to the search for spiritual truth.

In the late 1990's Phillip and I were consumed by the *Conversations with God* books by Neale Donald Walsch. We eagerly awaited each new book in the series. The CWG books revealed a God infinitely wise and accessible, even funny, who explained creation free of biblical and institutional church jargon or dogma, unlike anything I had learned from scripture, my church or a priest. I knew in my heart this was liberating, joyful truth, and I was hungry for more.

We attended a workshop with Neale at the Omega Institute in Rhinebeck NY. Neale and Phillip really clicked. Neale was attracted by Phillip's high-powered marketing experience and assertive style, since he was looking to expand his international profile through his best-selling books. I wrote a few articles about Neale and conducted a team building seminar for his staff in Oregon. For a time, it looked like the three of us might work together, but it soon became apparent we were not a good fit. I was disappointed when prospects for an exciting new spiritual path suddenly evaporated.

But a new spiritual path was about to unfold. Summer 2002 we attended a Unity church retreat in which we learned about a hands-on healing practice called Reiki. We found our way to Reiki Master Robert Baker, who, synchronistically, was about to begin a Reiki training program. Our training with Robert, which lasted several years, was the first step on a new spiritual journey that was to change our lives forever.

In his mid-fifties, Robert was blond, curly haired, almost cherub like, with a gentle speaking style. His Reiki classes comprised the first four steps in a much larger twelve-step Light Ascension program that he and his partner Ron Baker created with guidance from Archangel Gabriel. A critical part of the program involved working with Robert in a one-on-one personal process. I began to explore the questions of my life at a much deeper level than ever before.

We soon learned Robert channeled the Archangel Gabriel. I wasn't sure what that meant, but I was eager to find out. Robert conducted public sessions with Gabriel every Sunday evening in his apartment. (I describe my first experience with Gabriel in, *The Second Coming, The Archangel Gabriel Proclaims* a *New Age,* Amazon.com.)

It's one thing to read about the teachings of a divine figure; it is quite another to talk with them. The people gathered in Robert's living room seemed familiar with Gabriel and didn't act as though talking to him was a big deal. Fifteen years later, I still feel the powerful effect Gabriel had on me.

In time, at Phillip's urging, I suggested to Robert I write a book based on my interviews with Gabriel. We were frustrated that the questions posed at the Sunday sessions were mainly about personal issues and problems. That was understandable, but I wanted to learn more about creation and spiritual truths. Robert and Gabriel both agreed to work with me, and *The Second Coming* is the result. I treasure the years Gabriel patiently answered my countless questions about God and creation that ultimately filled a 340-page book. Sadly, Robert Baker left this dimension in 2013. All of us who knew that loving soul miss him greatly.

CHAPTER 3:
SACRED JOURNEYS

———

While working on *The Second Coming*, I joined two sacred journeys with Children of Light, the spiritual group Robert Baker and his spiritual partner Ron Baker founded based on Gabriel's teachings. The first was to Burma in 2003, coinciding with the Harmonic Concordance, a spiritual event initiated by a planetary alignment forming a six-point star in the sky, a stunning sight I will never forget. Gabriel created a series of complex rituals we were to follow which were designed to help "awaken the world's soul."

November 8, 2003 was the date of the Harmonic Concordance, which also happened to be my late partner Adam's birthday. I felt very much the novice as most members of our group had been on several previous sacred journeys. I did not really understand the significance of the rituals and assumed everyone else knew what was going on. My project with Gabriel had begun the previous April, and I was eager to have this spiritual experience.

Because this cosmic event was occurring on Adam's birthday, I hoped somehow to spiritually connect with him. The ritual began before sunrise on a large temple terrace high on a hill under a vast star-filled sky. As I studied the sky I was startled to clearly see a configuration of six planets forming a giant Star of David. Then the universe put on a vast, breathtaking cosmic show as an eclipse of the moon unfolded on one horizon while the sun rose on the other. We completed a long, complex ritual involving many changing partners, ending in the embrace of a final partner. My final partner's name was Adam.

I felt somewhat dazed by the experience. That evening as the group processed our day with Gabriel, I asked about my experience. Gabriel called it "a little joke from the universe." Laughter helped me lighten up and enjoy myself.

That worked until the sixth and final ritual when I encountered Merlin. On these spiritual journeys, Robert channeled many spiritual entities whose mission related to a particular ritual, activity or location. Merlin was one of the planetary incarnations of St Germain whom I had never heard of. Now I'm honored to say that St Germain calls me "beloved student, friend and colleague." I have learned that he is the great Ascended Master who is guiding mankind's ascension during this new 2000-year age of Aquarius. He has had many famous incarnations including Joseph, the Father of Jesus, Christopher Columbus and Francis Bacon whom, he says, was the true author of plays attributed to William Shakespeare. In the 5th century Merlin was the great alchemist, prophet and counselor at the court of King Arthur.

Merlin's voice roared out of Robert with a heavy Scottish accent, laughing and joking with a sarcastic, take-no-prisoners wit. I was somewhat startled since every entity I heard Robert channel spoke with Robert's much softer voice. Merlin seemed an entirely different being whom I found somewhat intimidating.

Each of us sat one at a time before Robert, who was seated on a chair in trance, while we dialogued with Merlin. Though Merlin kidded and joked and asked probing questions about what we were doing with our lives, he was reasonably courteous with each individual—until I sat before him.

In a somewhat mocking tone, he greeted me with, "Well, hello little man." I was a spiritual neophyte, and, as the oldest member of the group, I did not feel fully a part of it. With that sarcastic greeting in front of everyone and his challenging questions and comments, I felt embarrassed and confused by his hostility. I was consumed by feelings of unworthiness and not good enough that affected me for months. I felt very apprehensive about encountering Merlin again the following year on our next sacred journey to Egypt.

I don't have a transcript of my first encounter with Merlin in Burma, but I do have a transcript of my second meeting the following year in 2004 in Egypt. By this second meeting, I had been conversing with Gabriel for a year and felt more spiritually grounded and less insecure. Here is an excerpt from our conversation:

Merlin: And who stands before us now?

Joel: Joel does.

M: Goodness, back for more are you?

J: I guess so.

M: You are a glutton.

J: I guess.

M: So learn anything Joel since we last spoke with you?

J: I hope so.

M: So it has been a lovely year has it?

J: It has been a wonderful year.

M: Oh good. What would you say, is the most important thing you have uncovered about yourself?

J: One of the things I resented most about your comments last year was you said I kept myself under a bushel. I didn't like that at all.

M: And why was that?

J: There was probably more truth in that than I probably wanted to admit to.

M: Oh well, well. The path of the initiate is simply the path of truth because it is the path of the soul. And the soul doesn't lie—to itself or anyone else, for that matter, because it is so thirsty for life. And it is thirsty to nurture life in all of life. That has been challenging for you for your time. Like to hide away. Changed your stripes have you Joel?

J: Well, I think I'm in process.

M: Ah, you're willing to be humble about it. That's a step, Joel. Clever fellow, this Joel. Doesn't know how clever he is sometimes. So, Joel, you don't have conflicts, do you? Have it all figured out? If you were to entertain the idea, perhaps, that there might be a conflict in there, what do you imagine that it would be?

J: The idea of not being good enough and allowing that to be a stumbling block or a potential barrier.

M: Ah, so there is some wisdom in there after all. Thought so. So tell us, Joel, how important is this to you?

J: It's everything.

M: So are you willing to be entirely what you hate?

J: Yes, there is nothing else.

M: Perhaps your humility is not a mask after all. You see, Joel, in order to tread the path that you say you are choosing, you must be available to it. In order to be available to it you must sometimes be able to acknowledge with an open heart that you know nothing. What do you say to that?

J: I'm glad you're saying that because there are times when I feel that I know nothing after all this time.

M: Oh good. That is what has you trapped in time, knowing something. You see, knowledge has no use to you without the wisdom to use it. The wisdom to use it comes from knowing nothing. Now there's a riddle for you. Turn that around in your head or transform it in the heart. How do you feel, Joel, about being seen in the bright sun by the world?

J: I feel perfectly fine about it, if I believe it is expressing wisdom.

M: But what if you're not good enough?

J: I am good enough.

(We went back and forth several times repeating similar statements, which came to the issue of growing in consciousness.)

M: To do that (grow in consciousness) you'll have to embrace the "other" as well. This is your path; this is your conflict. Trying too hard to remain on one side creates an enemy of the other. Do you see? If you can embrace the other side, you can make your enemy your ally. This is a very important part of the initiate's journey because then and only then can you come to the place where you know nothing. Then you become wise.

Merlin had us pick a card at the end of our individual session. My card, titled Konsu, read:

"The challenge here involves being willing to go in new directions with enthusiasm. Let go of cynicism and have fun. Be willing to take a leap into the unknown."

M: What if you're not good enough?

J: I'm good enough.

M: No you're not. You can't go there if you are. You don't have to. We'll let you figure that out.

Everything you need to know is right there. (On the card.) Study it carefully. You may just be able to become not good enough. That is where your power is. Get it?

J: Got it. I had a much better time this year than last.

M: Oh really? You must have grown some then. Not so full of yourself.

I have to laugh when I read our discussion now. I see now that the fear of not knowing and not being good enough could keep me frozen in place, like a deer in the headlights, and stop me from fulfilling my life mission and destiny. I had to release my fear of the unknown, of not being good enough, if I were to muster the courage to "go in new directions with enthusiasm. Let go of cynicism and have fun. Be willing to take a leap into the unknown." If I wait to be fully prepared to step into the unknown, I will remain stuck, frozen in place.

Moreover, if I were "good enough" I wouldn't have to step into the unknown, because I "wouldn't have to." So accepting not being good enough becomes a qualification and a justification for the journey into the unknown.

We who go on these sacred journeys are often reminded that we are proxies for mankind, so Merlin's opening remarks (below) to our group before he began our individual sessions are really meant for all of us.

We were clustered near the base of the four towering figures of Ramesses II carved into the Great Temple at Abu Simbel overlooking the Nile River. As the brilliant sun faded towards the west, it felt as though we truly were a reunion of souls honoring an agreement we all had made long ago in some ancient time.

Greetings:

All the initiates are assembled, we assume, on this most officious occasion. This occasion where it is a day of thanksgiving in many ways and a day of relief in other ways as we understand that those who command the world at this time are vying for position.

You are in a place where the vying for position began, the sacred place of the ancient Egyptian gods and goddesses who once again make their archetypal visitation in this time when all the archetypes reveal their missions. Each of the sacred representatives of the ancient times of the legacy of Egypt and the ancient ones are all part of the star systems from which you have originated—and we as well.

*Since that time, we have been negotiating the plan for the evolution of this time to bring all of you into a place of readiness—readiness for the next stage—**unification of your wonderful adventure called life**.*

Those of you present on this day have chosen to be so. Therefore, as you speak with us and as we play together on this day as you enter into a negotiation with life that will be much different for you than any previous experience that you have had, from this day forward your inability, supposedly, for not being able to take responsibility for your lives and for the lives of your fellow compatriots will no longer be excused. So there!

We are known by some as the ancient visitor, Merlin. To some we are known as a prankster, a jokester. To others we are known as a sorcerer. To others as a revered teacher. So have some respect. Not too much, but have some—that we know a little bit about that of which we speak, and that we have some foresight. Otherwise, we would not have the job.

It is most important the job that you are about to embark upon in this new age of your time. For it is an agreement that you have made, where the souls that make up this planet are concerned, in your time, a long, long time ago.

You're only now, as you sit here before me and we before you, remembering what we have agreed to do. That we have agreed, all of us, to come play our various roles on the contract that we made, as we decided to be a part of this glorious and grand experiment called Earth life, called physical experience, whereby an intergalactic movement begins.

*You are the seeds of that movement. You are the first planet— as many of you have been told by other spiritual entities that have come through this channel—that you are part of a great plan that brings together twelve star-seeds into a single operation called planet Earth. **And on this planet, you have decided to awaken God in this experience.***

What you see here in this ancient place is the prophecy of this time. It is a prophecy of awakening all of the archetypes of that evolution into your godliness, into the nobility of your physical experience.

*So we are here to initiate with you the next steps to prepare you the way, so to speak. As we do so, we work with you to prepare you by consulting with you from the deepest part within you to **address that which keeps you from allowing yourself to become the great beings that you are, that addresses the deepest heart of your limitations that causes your heart to remain as a protective vehicle rather than one that can experience all that is.***

Our intent and goal is to facilitate that matter, and in doing so, we will be quite ruthless. As the parent always says to the child, it is for your highest good.

We have, because of our position in the hierarchy in service, if you will, consulted your soul design so that we could see where each person is in their readiness, and we also could see what their greatest challenge is at this time that they must meet in order to come into that which they are already.

Let us not waste further time with our chatter. Let us begin and commence on this journey together, this journey of testing the initiates, to see whether their readiness to choose is indeed sincere, is indeed aware, is indeed consciously chosen. For an unconscious choice will get you into more trouble than you care to be in.

Let us begin. We will ask that you volunteer from your own hearts as when you would like to proceed from us. Don't hold back. Step up, step up. Let us begin the circus. Let the games begin.

As I have observed, Merlin helped me discover that it was my fear of not being good enough—perhaps rooted in my childhood—that had turned my heart into a "protective vehicle rather than one that could *experience all there is*." That crippling fear kept me (and keeps many of us) from being the "great being" that Merlin says I/we are.

Love and fear, which is the absence of love, were central to the teachings I was receiving from Archangel Gabriel.

CHAPTER 4:
ARCHANGEL GABRIEL

My adventure with Gabriel had begun a year before the 2004 trip to Egypt. I saw our discussions as an opportunity to learn all about creation from an "infallible" Source. However, Gabriel said the primary benefit was my *own growth*, which would then be shared with others through my writing and teaching. Only now, in retrospect, can I see how true that is. Gabriel has been a great gift to my spiritual awakening.

My interviews with Gabriel continued through 2005. Most were conducted by telephone. Robert taped the two-hour discussions and mailed them to me. Each session took some 20 hours to transcribe. Over the next few years I edited, proofed and organized a pile of transcripts. Gabriel spoke in long sentences I called angelese. My challenge was to edit them down to clear, understandable sentences without altering his meaning and then to organize the material into a logical series of subjects for the manuscript which I published in 2008.

We discussed a vast range of topics including God, creation, evolution, mankind's origins and history, Jesus and other ascended masters, religion, scripture, health and healing, death, sexuality, government and even the U. S. invasion of Iraq, which was a hot topic at the time.

I can see now that Gabriel's teachings laid the foundation for this book, *The Refounding of America.* Gabriel revealed the critical role the United States of America is playing in mankind's spiritual evolution in this excerpt from my introduction to *The Second Coming:*

Mankind on earth is part of a divine experiment, which Gabriel says is unique in the universe. He indicates the earth was seeded millions of years ago by twelve star-systems that created the human form (humans are unique in the universe) as a vehicle to allow God to experience the ascension of the soul, with twelve archetypes of the divine being represented by those twelve star-systems. The ascension is an evolutionary process of the discovery of the God within each one of us (our souls) that gives God the opportunity to "experience twelve aspects of the divinity of the force of love."

Each of us as a soul has chosen to come here from one of the twelve star-systems to participate in this experiment. Many spiritual masters have come to help in that process, including Jesus whose birth Gabriel announced two thousand years ago. Jesus, Gabriel says, demonstrated the pattern of self-mastery that produces the awakening and the ascension of the soul in man through a series of "initiations," the seven stages of soul evolution (birth, baptism, transfiguration, renunciation, crucifixion, resurrection and ascension) that Christian religions recognize but don't completely understand.

Now Gabriel is proclaiming a new two-thousand-year age, the age of spiritual unity of all mankind. This new age was born on January 23, 1997, signaled by a configuration of planets aligned to form a six-point star—the same configuration Gabriel says announced the birth of Jesus two thousand years ago.

In this new age, mankind will follow the pattern Jesus demonstrated to awaken the soul, the Christ Consciousness, in each one of us. This, he says is the Second Coming. It is "not the Christ, the man, coming to rescue and save you. That is a fallacy. What he was telling you was that the Christ lies within you. You are the Christ. The time in evolution has come for the Christ Consciousness, the soul, to awaken in all humankind. We come to give you the step-by-step process for the awakening of the Christ Consciousness in all humanity."

Preparation for this new age of unity of all mankind began centuries ago. A key component was the creation of the United States, which was to be the New Jerusalem, the promised land, the "land of the awakening of the new spirit," signified, Gabriel says, by the fact that the letters USA are the central letters in the word Jerusalem. "Its original intention was to be a synthesis of all the people of the world who have lived under oppression and have come here to find spiritual freedom and expression of their individual being. In its original intention, it was supposed to have been a collective of that democratic idea of the freedom of speech, freedom of religion, freedom of individual social construct, so that every person and every group can live together in harmony and peace.

"That creates a collective consciousness that brings together a synthesis of all the peoples around the globe to begin to synthesize all the belief systems into a new world of spiritual development. A new world that takes bits and pieces of everything and creates a synthesized whole to lead the world into a new level of unity, oneness, communion and spiritual freedom."

The United States, in essence, is the prototype of the unity that is to develop in mankind in this new two-thousand-year age.

But that has been "distorted," Gabriel warns, because our democracy is now dominated by huge global concentrations of wealth and power that have greatly reduced the power and influence of the individual, which is fundamental to the success of democratic societies. It is the few "seeking through their greed to control and dominate the many, rather than creating for the many an experience of equality and provision, support, compassion, love and prosperity."

These powers are working to undermine mankind's unity by fostering conflict, separation and disunity by gaining control through fear. "Create that war on terrorism, keep them fearful," he says, is a current manifestation of this strategy. He tells us to "wake up" because our leaders have been "bought and sold" by these powerful international consortiums. We must take back our democracy through the power of one—first alone, and then together in unity.

This unity will happen, he says, whether it happens on planet or off because it is "God's evolutionary plan." We are given the gift of free will. We have the power to create a "new golden age or a nuclear holocaust." It is up to us.

Nearly fifteen years after Gabriel spoke these warnings, we are in the second year of Donald Trump's presidency, and Gabriel's words seem prophetic: "These powers are working to undermine mankind's unity by fostering conflict, separation and disunity by gaining control through fear."

Even before his presidency, Mr. Trump was "undermining mankind's unity" by stoking fear and demonizing Mexicans, immigrants, Muslims, our free press and judiciary and attacking our relationships with our commercial trading partners. He has since aligned himself with dictators and strongmen and disparaged long-standing economic and mutual defense agreements with our democratic partners.

His administration sees "the world not as a global community but an arena where nations and businesses engage and compete for advantage." In other words, his is a voice of separation, not the "unity of God's evolutionary plan."

These, indeed, seem the "darkest of times" as St Germain observed, "threatening to destroy the democratic foundations on which the nation was built."

Now what?

St Germain tells us that long ago the forces of creation set the intention to create a world based upon love, a reflection of creation itself. That reflection is still coming into focus through a nation with a government of the people, by the people and for the people: the United States.

But St Germain also tells us, these "darkest of times" are another great test in the history of a nation that promised love, equality, harmony and balance to itself and the world. Transmuting the dark forces and restoring the original mission will require a grand awakening of the people.

Awakening to what? The divine mission of United States, which is to bring love, peace, equality, harmony and balance to the world through a government based on *we the people*. To accomplish this mighty task, we the people must *be* love, peace, equality, harmony and balance.

Looking at the state of our country and humanity today, it's fair to ask, how in the world can we accomplish that?

Gabriel and I talked a lot about this challenge in *The Second Coming*. I had observed that one of the *Conversations with God* books quotes Jesus as saying, "Love one another as you would yourself..." and God finished the sentence, "because it is yourself."

Gabriel responded: "Yes. We would also say, love one another as you are able to love yourself. What you cannot accept and embrace within yourself, you will not be able to accept and embrace in another. So, if you are not able to accept and embrace all parts of yourself, how are you going to accept and embrace all parts of the individual whole?

"You have to create peace and harmony and acceptance within yourself before you can do that with others. It is important that you integrate you first, that you do your internal process to be at peace with you and awaken the soul in you. Then you can love another. You can only love another as you love yourself. If you cannot love yourself, you cannot love one another because you're only having one relationship and that is a relationship with yourself.

"If you are in duality with yourself and not in full acceptance of yourself, how can you possibly be in full acceptance of others? If you are not able to integrate the wholeness of your individuality and respect and honor it and experience the integrity of it, how can you ever possibly expect to do that with the individuality of everyone else?"

When I asked Gabriel how we can learn to fully accept ourselves, he responded, "By dealing with all of your past history. Dealing with all the traumas and conflicts within you. Dealing with everything within yourself that divides you from loving yourself and accepting yourself unconditionally and completely. And being able to separate, reveal and share every part of your being without reservation and without judgment. How many parts of yourself are you able to accept? What are the parts of yourself that you hide that you are ashamed you cannot accept? What feelings within yourself do you find difficult to embrace and accept and respond to? These are all parts of yourself from which you are divided, all parts of yourself you have disowned or suppressed or judged or shamed. All that needs to be owned, to be brought into integration. All that needs to be healed."

So all parts of us we've disowned, suppressed, judged or shamed need to be integrated, owned and healed. That is our challenge, our journey, Gabriel said.

No problem. Actually, I didn't have a clue how to do that.

One place I could start the healing process was with my sexuality, which, as far as I was concerned, was a core issue that affected almost every aspect of my life, especially my ability to love myself. So I was eager to ask Gabriel about it. In 2003 Pope John Paul II called homosexuality evil and condemned gay marriage. I asked Gabriel, what he would say to the pope who claims to have infallibility with regard to matters of spirit?

"You know nothing about spirit!" Gabriel responded. "Spirit embraces all being. It embraces the soul's individuation of being in all forms."

Embrace all beings (souls) in all their forms.

In other words, love ourselves and one another. That is how we begin to integrate, own and heal all the parts of us that we have disowned, suppressed, judged and shamed. That is how we heal, ourselves, humanity and the world. Love one another. That, of course, is a very old teaching. But we can't love another unless we can love ourselves. How do we love ourselves if we have been taught not to?

Divine wisdom about that healing process was about to be revealed to me by another archangel. His name was Michael.

CHAPTER 5:
ARCHANGEL MICHAEL

I conducted my first interview with Gabriel for the Second Coming on April 11, 2003. Phillip sat in the room quietly listening. By the end of the decade he was anything but quiet and appeared to be turning into a spiritual tuning fork. He had become a channel for Archangel Uriel and a growing host of higher realm beings, including someone by the name of Adama. I don't mean to be flip, because Adama turned out to be the father of mankind, and, as I have hinted, someone of great import to me.

Phillip tells the story of his spiritual development in this first book, *Coming Home to Lemuria*, a tale of our spiritual mission in 2010 to Mt. Shasta, the earthly home of St Germain, Adama and the remnants of the ancient civilization of Lemuria.

Phillip by now had retired from commercial film production and was turning his considerable energies to spiritual studies and work. He helped organize five of us who were members of Robert's spiritual group, Children of Light, into a group of our own, which we called Children of the Awakened Heart (COTAH.)

One of the members, Jeff Fasano, channeled the Archangel Michael, whose teachings are designed to help us live through our knowing hearts rather than our believing minds. We soon began organizing our group around Michael's teachings, which committed us to Five Agreements which he called Guidelines for Living. The agreements appear deceptively simple. As I sought to apply them, they gradually helped me rethink my priorities and reshape my life.

Here are Archangel Michael's Five Agreements:

Agreement 1: Commit to World service.

World service is our mission and the foundation of our work. It is an agreement to use our gifts and talents to raise the level of resonance and vibration in the world in order to create a new world of community, harmony and equality.

Agreement 2: Commit to a personal process.

This agreement asks us to process our personal issues that hold us in lack and limitation because of old patterns, attachments and behaviors. A personal process is designed to help us move from "Me" consciousness to "We" consciousness so that we may develop healthy relationships with a balance of giving and receiving. A personal process helps us to know who we are and to develop a strong sense of self, so we may develop our gifts and talents and take them out to the world to serve mankind.

Agreement 3: Focus on "what is" in our lives.

Focusing on what *is* focuses our consciousness on what we are grateful for, which engages the formula Gratitude = Abundance. Focusing on what is *not* traps us in a cycle of perpetual discontent, causing us to ignore our internal resources and seek fulfillment outside ourselves. We then risk missing the "diamonds in our own backyard" and the opportunities they represent.

Agreement 4: Develop a sense of self.

This is an agreement to move into the depth of our *hearts* to honor, value and love ourselves—essential qualities if we are to achieve our full potential as human beings. When we know, love and honor ourselves, we are better prepared to identify, develop and offer our gifts and talents in service to the world. It is the deep love of the self that *powers* our ability to *be* who we are.

Agreement 5: Receive love.

If love powers our ability to be who we are, then we need to learn to give love to ourselves, rather than constantly seek it from others. When we learn to love ourselves, we do not make others responsible for loving us. That frees us to love others unconditionally without the insatiable needs of the wounded self. We can then be the person we choose to be, create our own path and develop healthy relationships reflecting a balance of giving and receiving.

I worked as a management and human development consultant for many years. Michael's focus on the importance of self-love was totally consistent with behavioral science. People with high levels of self-esteem—who love, honor and respect themselves—tend to be happy and successful. They are likely to be clearer about their goals, have the drive to achieve them and are able to develop healthy, balanced professional and personal relationships.

However, behavioral scientists also understand that meaningful life change doesn't tend to come from simply becoming *aware* of healthy behavior. It requires mindful *practice*—practicing new behaviors until they become *additions* to one's natural behavior repertoire. The Five Agreements, valuable as they are, provide general guidelines for living happier, fulfilling lives. We needed to learn how to *implement* them. Michael was about to teach us how.

Phillip began having internal discussions with Adama, the high priest of Telos, a Lemurian City under Mt. Shasta in Northern California, which Phillip describes in *Coming Home to Lemuria*. According to Adama, Lemuria was a vast continent that was destroyed by Atlantis in a nuclear holocaust and disintegrated under the Pacific Ocean some 12,000 years ago. A group of survivors led by Adama evacuated to Mt. Shasta, preserving the civilization's records for future generations.

Phillip summarized the story in this excerpt from *Coming Home to Lemuria*:

> *The Lemurians knew well in advance of the impending demise of their world. Thus, they were able to use their crystalline energy technology to create a massive underground city (Telos) where they could preserve their culture not only for themselves, but also for those of us who would live in the Earth in the future. Without their efforts at preservation those on the surface could never return "home" to a higher frequency existence.*

> *About twenty-five thousand Lemurians managed to migrate to the interior of Mount Shasta before the Atlanteans destroyed their home on the surface. Adama told me, "We currently exist in light bodies that are not constrained by the limitations of your physical world. Someday you will join us in this fifth-dimensional reality. Your Mother Earth has already begun to shift her frequency, and all things within and upon her body will shift. This is your destiny."*

> *Adama reported that the Lemurian civilization existed on the surface for millions of years. They mastered electron energy and telepathy eons ago. "We have technological abilities that make your 3D abilities look like child's play. We control most of our crystalline and amino acid technologies with*

our minds. We can travel through space and have the ability to make our spaceships invisible and soundless to avoid detection by your military.

"Many of your world leaders know we exist; however, they are keeping this fact from you. Although we are physical beings, we can shift our energy fields from the third to the fifth dimensional frequency and be visible or invisible at will. This will prevent the inhabitants of your world from harming us until the time when you are ready to know and accept us. The time is coming for our two civilizations to merge."

None of us in COTAH suspected we were about to take an important step toward making that merger a reality. Coincidentally, we learned Archangel Michael had played a major role in the establishment and development of the Lemurian culture.

All five of us had gone on sacred journeys with Robert Baker, so it wasn't a stretch for Phillip to suggest that we as a group take a sacred journey to Mt Shasta in California. We jumped at the idea, no small reason because it was not in some far-off exotic location like previous journeys.

We consulted Michael about the journey. He responded, "Yes, dear ones, there is a very important mission to be accomplished on Mount Shasta, and the five of you will serve as proxies for humankind to achieve that mission. When you are there you will open a gateway between the Lemurians below ground and those of us in the fifth dimension above. This event will assist in balancing the feminine and masculine energies on your planet; it will enable you to balance receiving and giving. The planet is shifting into balance and everything within and upon her body must also shift."

The next day Phillip received this confirmation from Adama:

The time has come for us to connect directly. Each one of you brothers of the awakened heart are being prepared to do so, if you so choose. You have connected with the Lemurians through the heart energy of your beloved Michael, for only through your hearts can you connect with the fifth dimension. Situations are happening faster than even we Lemurians thought possible. Much is in the process of being revealed to your world. Other worlds and realities are coming forth, and humankind is almost ready to receive the truth. We dwell in your inner planet, safe from your density and separation. We are assisting in your awakening to the truth of your being from below and from above, from your archangelic and star realms. The above and below are meeting in your hearts, dear ones, bypassing your minds.

This change is more change than your world has ever seen from the unseen. For it is time. The time has come for humankind to know who you are and why you are here, and this begins with each and every one of you individually. Your beloved Michael is teaching you this, as this realm created and taught us. You are finally awakening to the divinity within you and to remember that you are eternal life force light connected to the creator.

Your impending sacred journey to our inner home, Mount Shasta, is a journey the five of you are being guided to receive by us and Michael. Others shall follow. You have prepared for this journey your entire life and even before. The work and exercises that you are presently involved in doing with Michael are essential prior to this trip. That is why Michael is guiding you to do them. Only through the healing of yourself can you heal your world and receive our reality, the new world order.

This is the precious opportunity for your world that shall not come again soon. You chose to be here now to assist in the necessary shift. Again, it is essential that you do the work on yourself to remove yourself from yourself in order to move into the We. The world the Lemurians live in is all about the We, for the We is all there is. Your veils are being lifted to see us and the truth. You are beings of light and must return to the light. Your planet has already done so. Thus, all things within and upon your planet must do so also. Those who choose otherwise shall dwell in another reality elsewhere, if necessary.

We love you beyond your present love of self and are as anxious to meet you, as you are to meet us. But you must be ready. Are you ready? We must meet at a similar frequency, and that requires you coming to us. We await you.

In *Coming Home to Lemuria* Phillip describes in great detail our unforgettable week on Mt. Shasta in May 2010, including messages he received from Adama and the messages and the rituals Jeff received from Michael and other spiritual entities.

Again, as in Burma and Egypt, I participated in the rituals without really understanding the energetic connections we were creating. Nor did I feel the energies to the degree reported by Phillip, our three companions or our guide Ashalyn. "Don't compare your experience with others," Michael counseled, but I still felt less spiritually connected to the experience unfolding on the mountain. In truth, I felt less spiritually worthy.

However, I did connect powerfully with the teachings Michael asked us to review as part of our preparation for the Shasta trip. Jeff had channeled this material a few years before. I saw immediately that these were powerful teachings for our personal growth and development. Later, I came to realize here were the teachings we needed to not only make the Five Agreements a powerful reality in our lives; they also offered the potential for great personal healing.

Of this wisdom, Adama said, "Only through the healing of yourself can you heal your world and receive our reality, the new world order."

After the Mt Shasta trip, I adapted and organized Michael's teachings into a format similar to my corporate training programs and conducted several workshops in New York and Ft. Lauderdale where I spend my winters. I published the program as *Life Mastery, A Guide for Creating the Life You Want and the Courage to Live It* (Amazon).

Michael's teachings, I believe, fully achieve their mission to "help you achieve your full potential as a human being." Michael's welcoming message to students provides the context for understanding Life Mastery's intentions and healing power.

A MESSAGE FROM ARCHANGEL MICHAEL

We welcome you, as you are now ready to move into a new life of community, harmony and equality.

Whether or not you know it consciously, you have reached the point where you are ready, open and available to receive what you say you want.

This is not necessarily anything outside of you that validates or gratifies you. It is something that resonates within you.

Some who are reading this understand fully why you are here, and some of you are just getting a glimpse of it.

*The important thing is that you are ready to find within you the answer to **where you are going in the world.***

*As you begin the process of exploration in this program, we begin by asking, why are you here? Are you here to get something for yourself? Are you here just to get by, endure life and survive? **Or are you here to move out into the world to express your gifts and talents?***

*In your **heart** you know the answers, and it is time to take the next step.*

*You are here for the purpose of **world service**.*

Loving who you are and what you do and bringing that out into the world is world service.

*The answers to how you can do that are in your **heart**. That is why this program is designed to take you on a journey from the core of your **mind** into the core of your **heart**.*

The messages and exercises contained within this program are tools to be utilized while making this journey.

*As you begin reading the first message in lesson one, you will begin a process of allowing your **heart** to become the guiding force of your life. For some, the shift in consciousness that makes this possible is gradual. For others, it is sudden.*

*The process involves peeling layer upon layer of **wounding** from around your heart until you have moved **into** your heart and uncovered the essence of your truth. As you release each layer of wounding that surrounds your heart, you will also raise the level of **resonance** and **vibration** within you.*

*This occurs because each layer of wounding is filled with lower vibration energy, which simply represents what you have learned during childhood about how to **survive** in the world and how you were **conditioned.***

The intention of this program is to begin to peel away these layers of wounding.

As you progress through the lessons, you will discover your talents and gifts, and you will realize that your purpose in life involves giving those talents and gifts to the world in ways that bring you fulfillment and joy.

*By engaging in this process of self-discovery, you will raise the level of resonance and vibration in your **self**.*

*As you accomplish this, you will raise the level of resonance and vibration of the **world,** thus helping to co-create a new world of community, harmony and equality.*

Here are some key teachings from the program:

PRINCIPLES OF LIFE MASTERY

1. Let your love for yourself power your courage to be you.

2. Break old habits and patterns that keep you in lack and limitation.

3. Release attachments that do not serve your highest good.

4. Think with your heart. Your heart will guide you to your place in the world.

5. Observe what *resonates* for you (how you feel) and develop *discernment* (how you think) to choose what serves your highest good.

6. Discover your gifts and talents and joyful ways to employ them.

7. Decide what you want. (You are either having what you want or you are avoiding a feeling—fear, etc.)

8. Release fear. Fear is an illusion. It has no life of its own but the energy you give it. Feel your fear and do what resonates and you discern—anyway.

9. Harness the power of *intention* and the *word.* Intentions give direction to your life, and your words can empower or disempower.

10. Be willing to step into the unknown—where creation takes place.

11. Don't try to fit in. Make your mark in the world by fully acknowledging your unique gifts, talents and personal qualities—and fly.

12. Develop healthy relationships with a balance of giving and receiving.

13. Set your boundaries.

14. See challenges as opportunities for learning and growth.

15. Let joy guide you forward on your path.

I conducted my first Life Mastery program as I was approaching my 75th birthday. As they say, teach what you need to learn. I began to explore the questions of who am I and why am I here at deeper levels than I had never explored them before. Better late than never.

To repeat, Life Mastery is intended to help us develop our full potential as human beings. Shortly before I created the Life Mastery program, I had begun a relationship with two divine beings who desired to reach out to those of us who wish to know ourselves as far *more* than human. *The Ascension Handbook* was created for those who seek to know themselves as *God*.

Gabriel told me many times that we humans are individual expressions of God. The Two Marys helped me to truly *hear* it.

CHAPTER 6:
THE TWO MARYS

I met the Two Marys on May 5, 2010, a few weeks before we left on our Mt. Shasta trip. The Two Marys are the combined energies of Mary, the mother of Jesus, and Mary Magdalene, Jesus' spouse and twin flame.

I have always felt a powerful connection to the Virgin Mary. As a child of the Catholic Church, I regularly said the rosary, attended novenas and was fascinated by the stories of Mary's appearances at Lourdes, Garabandal and other locations around the world. I traveled twice to Medjugorje, Yugoslavia in the late 1980's where Mary was reported to be appearing to some young people. I met several of them and prayed intensely, but I felt little connection to the physical location, which was visited by thousands of faithful pilgrims.

Years later, seemingly out of nowhere, another profound spiritual adventure—this time with the Mary energies—suddenly presented itself. Once again, the connection was through Phillip. *The Ascension Handbook*, published in 2011 was a collaboration between the Two Marys, channel Jessie Keener and me. I described our first encounter in my introduction to the Handbook:

This wonderful project began at lunch with Jessie Keener in spring 2010 in Fort Lauderdale, Florida. Jessie and I had been introduced by an old friend, Phillip Collins, who, with Jessie, had co-founded the Modern Day Mystery School in Fort Lauderdale. I led a book discussion group at the school on my book, The Second Coming, The Archangel Gabriel Proclaims a New Age. Jessie and I were becoming good friends. It didn't hurt that she loved my book. During lunch, Jessie told me that she channeled the Two Marys, the combined energies of Mother Mary and Mary Magdalene. I didn't know what that meant, but I sure wanted to find out.

With Jessie serving as the channel, I had my first conversation with the Two Marys (that is what they said to call them) in May 2010. I was embraced by the most powerful energy of love I have ever experienced. It wasn't until March 2011 that the Two Marys revealed that our project would be a "series of intelligent articulations regarding the human conundrums with Ascension."

I had no idea what that meant, but The Ascension Handbook is the result. It is truly what the subtitle says, A Guide to Your Ecstatic Union with God. I love the Two Marys. I love what they teach humankind about this powerful time of Ascension. I am honored that they chose to work with me. And I hope they give me another job.

My story, like many of our stories, is about rising consciousness. My spiritual conversations up to that point had been with archangels who were rather formal in answering my questions. I was not expecting the warm, loving, personal conversations I had with the Two Marys, which were often sprinkled with laughter. Nor did I expect the revelations that began with our first conversation, the first of many over the next few years.

These are the first words the Two Marys spoke to me May 5, 2010:

Greetings beloved Joel:

We are delighted that we are attuning with your presence this evening. We salute you. We are the Two Marys and we are here to give you guidance, love and support as you continue on your journey to your heart, through your heart, out into the world.

We have a brief message for you and then we will allow you to ask questions which we know you have.

It brings us great joy to say that we are proud that you have come this far in this lifetime and accomplished what you have in your work. We want you to know, because often it is overlooked or understated around you and to you, that you have made enormous progress.

We have been with you at many times throughout many incarnations. We want you to know we understand the sacrifices that you have been making, especially in the last seven to ten years of your time.

Your work has actually just begun in that you will continue to produce manuscripts and many, many writings. For you have been a scribe before, dear Joel. You were a scribe in the time of Jesus. You walked alongside the Two Marys for a brief while. You have always been close to our energies. This lifetime your writings will serve thousands and eventually millions. For that is your destiny. The undertaking of your future work, the Life Mastery, is most essential for your lifetime to do this work, to teach this work and to train others to teach this work. For teaching and training others is what our beloved Jesus did, did he not?

He developed a team and he taught that team how to duplicate his messages. In the beginning they were simply repeating the message. Gradually, as it filtered through their ego state into their heart state, they became the message. They became wide open conduits for all of the love that there is, and that is your destiny, Joel.

You have chosen to surround yourself with people who you call your soul family who will protect you as necessary to preserve your abilities to be free to be the scribe, to be the person with the writing, for your written words will heal many. It is important for us, as the Two Marys, to bring this to your full attention—not because of some ego state for you to become pleased with—rather for you to become self-aware as the messenger who truly has the gift.

So it is with great blessing and benediction that we salute you and acknowledge you. We remind you that we have walked with you and will continue to walk with you. At times you can feel us holding you gently. We will walk arm and arm, dear Joel. You will write for the masses. We salute you.

I felt bathed in love, though my head was spinning from their statement that we had walked together many times, including the time of Jesus. We continued our conversations periodically, but our work on The Ascension Handbook (Amazon) did not begin until April 2011. Because they dictated most of the content, we were able to publish the Handbook by year end. In their introduction, the Two

Marys explained what our Ascension Process is about and how the Handbook serves it.

Beloved Students:

You chose this lifetime as the culmination of all that you have ever been. You chose this lifetime whether you understand all your previous lives or not. You chose this lifetime to fully access God in your body, through your body and into what we call the Ascension Process.

We are the Two Marys, and we have entwined our frequencies as the Two Marys in this expression for the purpose of supporting you, beloved students, in fully realizing yourselves as God. This is called the Ascension Process—ascending from a limited awareness of what it means to be alive as a human and expanding that into the understanding that, indeed, you are God.

The Two Marys are the enjoining of the Mother Mary and Mary Magdalene at a very specific frequency for the purpose of assisting humanity in Ascension. As you read these words, we invite you into this exact frequency. If you choose, give yourself permission to enter this frequency of Ascension, for you have everything to gain and nothing to lose.

What we mean by this is you have spent lifetime after lifetime striving to serve your spiritual blueprint, striving to serve your soul's desire for unity, striving to become God. Now we are here to assist. Entering this frequency means you lose nothing. It means that you are open to very specific assistance from this fifth-dimensional frequency. We wish to introduce ourselves the following way: we are the entwining of Mother Mary, the Mother of Jesus, and Mary Magdalene, the twin flame of Jesus.

Therefore, throughout this teaching the Christ Consciousness will permeate your existence, if you choose to invite this frequency. For those of you who have always resonated with the Christ Consciousness, welcome home. For those of you who find that information new, welcome. Welcome to your home. The Christ Consciousness is not about religion. It is about love. The Christ Consciousness says I am God. This is the same as all spiritual teachings. All spiritual teachings say the student is God. The exercises that have always been on your planet to assist the student in moving forward have always been for the purpose of demonstrating to the student that he is God.

All of the gurus who have ever walked on your planet, all of the avatars—whether Jesus, Buddha, Mohammed or many others—have taught the very same thing. Welcome to your Ascension, beloved students. That is not to say you have not already been diligently ascending, for many of you have been. And because you picked up this very book, because you are reading these very words, we acknowledge you. We acknowledge that in your heart you know that you belong in Ascension, that you belong to God, and God belongs to you.

We wish to impart this truth to you beloved students: GOD IS COUNTING ON YOU TO BE GOD.

That is all and nothing more. Consider that. Take a deep breath as you read that. Imagine to yourself, "What does it really mean that God is counting on me?" God's mission, God's plan, is to fully experience. Nothing more. Nothing less. God is all that is; therefore, God's mission is your being God.

As you read the discourses that we have given you in the Ascension Handbook, pay attention to the part of your mind that wants to argue about whether you are God. You will be given tools, information and wisdom, and you will be given choices. Ascension always involves choices. There are no "shoulds" in this handbook.

Our goal is to create a continuous process for you by which you can ascend. Here is the truth. You will ascend anyway. Your Ascension is guaranteed. The only question is when. If you desire Ascension NOW in your life, this is your book. If you feel that you have all the time in the world, perhaps this is not your book. For our purpose is to co-create Ascension with each and every student.

If the co-creation of your Ascension resonates with you, it is time to begin. It is time for you to learn about Ascension in this frequency. It is time to get to know yourself through this material. It is time for you to increase your capacity for self-love and for joy. It is time for you to experience ecstasy that you experience only when you are fully connected to God.

IT IS TIME TO RETURN TO YOUR TRUE NATURE AS GOD.

Yes, it is time for us all, *to get to know ourselves, to increase our capacity for self-love and for joy and to return to our true nature as God.*

I realize now that is what Phillip's and my work over the last several years has been about. We have been writing books, conducting discussions and interviews with a host of divine beings, broadcasting radio programs and have led workshops and classes all ultimately containing the central theme of returning to our true nature as God. (See Theangelnewsnetwork.com.)

Clearly, our work has helped prepare us to join St Germain on this great adventure called *The Refounding of America.* Perhaps only when we look back at the mosaic of our lives can we see the picture that slowly, piece by piece, gradually emerges over time—like the awakening of our consciousness.

CHAPTER 7:
ST GERMAIN

Since his retirement from commercial film production, Phillip's productivity writing spiritual books and teachings has been every bit as breathtaking as his record producing ground breaking, big budget television commercials. I have lost count of the books he has published in the last several years. In the preface of one I wrote, "Phillip seems to produce spiritual books at the speed some great chefs produce superb cuisine."

As I reported earlier, St Germain announced during a friend's birthday party in October 2016 (with Phillip as channel) that we would collaborate on a project beginning in 2017 if we chose. I had no idea what the project was to be, but within a few weeks Phillip had already channeled a book titled, St Germain's Seven Ascension Discourses (See Part III). In addition to seven chapters of wisdoms on ascension, the material included a glossary of at least 600 teachings, terms and tools.

Phillip and I planned to begin discussing the teachings in private sessions with St Germain in January 2017. However, St Germain made it known to Phillip he wanted to discuss the book's fourth discourse, Codes of Creation to Support Your Ascension, during our monthly public discussion program we called Divine Discussions

on December 15, 2016. This would be my first opportunity to speak
with St Germain about our new project.

In this first meeting, St Germain outlined the significance of
mankind's ascension process at this time, the key role of the United
States in Earth's spiritual evolution and the value of the material he
was presenting for those who choose to commit to their ascension.

> *Beloved students:*
>
> *We are gathered at this auspicious time within your
> planetary history and the history of your individu-
> ated soul plans. I, St Germain, come to you from the
> ascended mastership for the greatest dispensation to
> assist you at this time of challenge and turmoil.*
>
> *There has always been challenge and turmoil during
> your human 3D existence, even within the incarna-
> tional cycles that have been briefly shared with you
> that I have experienced similar to the ones that you
> have experienced yourselves. It is so important at this
> time that you remember and apply that your ascen-
> sion process is a process of inside out, not outside in.
> And all that is happening in your world is an oppor-
> tunity, a test, if you will, a testament for the choice
> you will make that your ascension process will be the
> priority of your life and that you will commit what-
> ever is necessary to that process.*
>
> *That is what is required. It cannot be a part-time job.
> It must become the focus for it to take place. Some
> of you will do it in this incarnational cycle. Some of
> you will do it in later incarnational cycles. For those
> of you who choose not to complete your ascension*

in the final 2000-year cycle of this planet, you will be given the opportunity to do it and be it elsewhere.

The reason that we have come at this time is we realize within the time consortium that you exist in now that it is very difficult for you to focus and to absorb and integrate large masses of information, even though my teachings exist in elaborated volumes galore. So I have chosen, and the channel that I am coming through has chosen as an aspect of this individual's soul plan, to present to you simplified, concise teachings called the seven discourses, which will be elaborated upon with dialogues within your new year 2017.

We realize that this is a challenging moment for humanity, particularly in these United States. Long before the United States actually existed, we within the ascended mastership realms had a divine design to create a platform for bringing We consciousness and equality, harmony and balance into existence within this planet. So we helped dictate, if you will, the founding father papers of these United States, which were amalgamations of what you had experienced in the past through your governments and your kingdoms, in combination with the fifth dimensional higher realm wisdoms, to create a platform, a way showing, of how to be an enlightened, wise nation and allow that wisdom to move out into your entire world.

It is the destiny of these United States, the Americas including what you call South America, to be these way showers. We are instrumental in making sure this happens.

We wish to assure you that the planet herself is protected by we of the ascended mastership and the other higher realms. It cannot and will not be destroyed by human activity. When that was attempted those particular advanced civilizations were destroyed themselves.

Through your freedom of choice and will, you will allow the pushing and pulling of your ascension process, as has been explained, not always in a straight line. Sometimes you take one or two steps forward, and then you may take some steps backwards in order to move forward.

The players upon the stage of your humanity, particularly of these United States, are upon the stage en-masse at this time to awaken humanity—and for those of you who resonate with a truly democratic, equal, harmonious and balanced civilization—to step forward like never before to learn and apply what is through the contrast of what is not. That is what you are creating and experiencing at this time in these United States.

It is all part of a divine plan, but it is up to you, individually, to not give up but to wake up and to step up to really reveal to yourself and to other like-minded and like-spirited communities of equality, harmony and balance who you truly are and why you truly are here.

*So let us begin with some of these tools we are going
to be focusing on tonight as you enter into your
Christ Consciousness season with Discourse 4.*

We spent the rest of the session discussing the 13 Codes of
Creation to Ascend contained in Discourse 4 designed to help us
raise our vibrations from the third dimension, where we now reside,
to the higher vibrations of the fifth dimension.

As this was my first significant exposure to St Germain, I was
eager to assess how he would be to work with. Every spiritual entity I
have worked with has their individual personalities. (To some degree
a channel's "filter" influences that personality.) Archangel Gabriel
patiently answered my every question (and my incessant follow-up
questions) and often brought a dry wit to his responses. The Two
Marys were very warm and nurturing. We often laughed together,
although they resisted discussing topics outside their ascension mission, such as my queries about every-day life with Jesus. Archangel
Michael was very serious, yet compassionate. I never managed to
elicit a hint of humor from him. His answers rarely strayed from the
personal process. He resisted commenting on other topics such as
current events.

In this first discussion, St Germain was very serious and busi-
ness-like, which was reinforced in our private sessions the following month. St Germain lets Phillip know in advance what he wants
to discuss, sticks to the agenda and resists straying from it. When
we're through, he's out of there.

I am most concerned about a spiritual entity's willingness to
answer my many questions and the clarity of their responses. Not
long into our discussion, St Germain's answers began to raise
my concerns.

The first Code of Creation states, *the higher realms have given us many tools to assist in the healing of our wounds and ego defenses.* I asked for examples of these tools. St Germain's answer referred to The Seven Discourses, the Inner Earth civilizations in the core of the planet, the star realms that seeded our planet and the inter-galactic realms that have a responsibility to this galaxy.

A tool is something we use to get a job done or to solve a problem. In what way are the Inner Earth civilizations, star realms, etc., tools, and how can they help heal our wounds and defenses? St Germain's answer was not clear or helpful to me. I hoped this (to me) incomplete and confusing answer would not be the norm. Repeatedly having to press a divine entity to clarify their answers makes it difficult to move spiritual wisdom from the abstract to the clear, which can weaken my work.

Yet, also in this first session, I encountered an extraordinary humility and a desire to bond with us I had never encountered in a spiritual entity. St Germain is serving as humanity's guide for this new 2000-year spiritual age of Aquarius, as Jesus did for the last spiritual age of Pisces. Despite his exalted state and mission, he confessed that before his ascension he struggled with many of the teachings he was giving us.

"Beloved students, I struggled with every one of these codes in every incarnational cycle that I have had. It's why I present them to you in the most simplified way possible through the channel. I do not wish them to be buried by a lot of spiritual dogma. I intend to present these as simply and concisely as possible and allow you to feel my connection with you as a way-shower to your destiny having been you. Can you feel that now? Can you feel your beloved St Germain reaching out to you to hold your hand, to caress your heart, in order to duplicate myself?

"That is my mission. That is the mission of every ascended master. We do not call ourselves masters. We simply replicate ourselves. If you really wish and intend to make your beloved St Germain happy, if you connect with my energy, which you do—I feel you—lets join in this ascension from this moment on unlike we ever have before."

I told St Germain that I had never heard a spiritual entity admit to the difficulties they faced in their own incarnational process, and it was empowering to hear that.

"That is our reason to be and do it at this time. We are not better than you are. We are you becoming me. Do you hear me? We're going into this in equality, harmony and balance from this moment forward. It is my intention to reveal a lot of what I went through in the process of becoming who I am as a part of sowing the way for you. It is time for that too!

"It is within the concept of oneness that I be this. Allow this truth for you to begin to access this concept of oneness a little more, perhaps, by our feelings for one another, of our love for one another. I am, you are, my brothers' and sisters' keepers, beloved students. The universe and creation and its planets are incomplete without every one of you. You've heard this, now know it, or you wouldn't be here."

This first discussion (12/15/16) with St Germain is a treasure of spiritual wisdom. The discussion occurred one month after the election of Donald Trump, and many citizens were already concerned with many of Trump's autocratic statements.

The second Code of Ascension reads, "My purpose is to learn to love through duality and to transcend into world service through unity. Lower frequencies are not allowed within the higher realms. My mission is to raise my frequency through consciousness."

I asked, "How do we raise our frequency through love when we are confronted with forces that might be stripping us of the gifts and freedoms you and other ascended masters have given us?"

St Germain responded that learning to be an ascended master is about learning to "master energy. We ask that you not go into it through resistance or to fight it, but to build a parallel path and butt it up next to it. See yourself creating this parallel path independent of what is happening in the density next to you. Allow that to be your commitment going forward, creating through the higher frequency of your energy the life you say you want of equality, harmony and balance.

"Creating the parallel path allows the existence you wish to live within, and that higher frequency, through the higher state of consciousness, will eventually negate and eliminate the denser frequency because you entrain, you rise to the highest frequency, the highest energy level, within the environment. So when you see something happening, whether it is an atrocity or a war or what you are experiencing in the United States at this time, we encourage you not to fall into resisting it. Build a higher vibration parallel path which eventually will eliminate the denser frequency.

"Every single thing that you call a war or an atrocity, in effect, is a clearing and a cleansing that is necessary for the way that humanity is choosing to learn. (Learning what *is* through what is *not*.) Remember, you can never die. You are an eternal spirit choosing to have a human experience on this planet at this time. There is a mission for this planet to master the force of love through duality and separation. Building a parallel path of higher vibration, instead of engaging with it, is one way to accomplish that."

Later in our conversation, St Germain shared these insights about the mission of planet Earth and humanity living upon her:

"This planet has the holiest, most divine purpose of any planet in creation. It is an amalgamation of everything good and bad, right or wrong, male and female, dark and light imaginable in creation all stirred up in one tiny blue-green ball flying hundreds of thousands of miles an hour through an endless, all-knowing space of probabilities and possibilities. You have chosen—in your formless, eternal spiritual being—to be a part of this divine experiment. Then, when it and you reach your ascension process, I wish to inform you that your real work, through all that there is, will begin anew.

"You will have experienced every aspect of what is *not* in order to know what *is* so that you will become love again—to bring that wisdom, that applied knowledge, out into many worlds, some less advanced than yours, some more advanced than yours. And you'll choose through your freedom of choice and will to repeat this as many times as you choose as the universe flies through the eternalness of it. This is who you are. This is why you are here, beloved students. You signed on to one of the greatest adventures in creation, coming to this planet and being human. Take a deep breath and know this aspect of yourself that you have never known before. In your deepest moments of fear, doubt and ignorance begin to tap into this truth that lies within your hearts. You are nothing more or nothing less than an expression of all that there is in all of your humanness.

"Each one of you is where you need to be. It has always been about you accepting this component of yourself (our divinity). It has been this you have feared the most. It hasn't been death; it hasn't been war. You have readily killed yourself and one another ad nauseum. We are weary of watching it, actually. What you truly fear is this (divine) spark because you have been taught in so many lifetimes it is otherwise by those who have attempted to control you with their lies, deception and deceit and their denial of the deceit.

Well, I am going to shine a little light on that, and together we will create a new paradigm, a new parallel paradigm. Are you ready?"

Yes, St Germain, I am ready to shine a light on the truth of who we truly are and create a new paradigm for mankind. I looked forward to our first private discussion in a few weeks.

CHAPTER 8:
FIRST PRIVATE SESSION

———

Our first private session started as a bummer. I did not have my new recorder ready to record our conversation when Phillip arrived at my apartment Monday morning, January 9, 2017. He was annoyed because he said he had difficulty accessing and holding St Germain's energy, so it was important to begin without delay.

When he came through Phillip, St Germain sounded annoyed as well, stating it was important to honor our appointments and to be prepared. (It was my first scolding by a divine being, and it did not feel good.) He said he would not be offering a teaching this first meeting but wanted to discuss what we would be doing together. He asked if I understood the purpose of the seven discourses and why we have chosen to present them in a public arena in addition to the private dialogues.

Joel: It's my understanding the discourses are a simplified version of teachings you have given previously and did not wish to repeat.

SG: It's not a matter of not wishing to repeat. It's a matter of what we have done in the past has not been working effectively. We are building a foundation so that what has preceded this can be more effective.

He explained that within the "duality, chaos, separation and confrontation" we on Earth live in, our work together would be a "preamble to self-mastery leading to ascended mastery." He said we on Earth would be going through a period of intensifying chaos which would "allow a clearing and cleansing to move into the mastership of the planet and humanity upon it.

"The seven discourses and glossary (Part III) offer a simplified, concise version of what has preceded and been previously received by humanity in great volumes. Because of the intensification of the ascension process of the planet and humanity upon and within the planet, there is a need for humanity to receive something in a simplified way with a more direct heart to heart, hand to hand connection, which is what I am intending to accomplish at this time."

St Germain said that through the rest of the year 2017 we would discuss the discourses and other teachings in public forums and private conversations and "you will bob and weave through all of this material through your resonance and discernment as to how you would like to proceed."

I asked St Germain about his teachings from the 1930's published by the St Germain Press, which I considered very powerful and empowering.

"Many of these sayings and mantras are trapped in the mental body of humanity and have not moved from the erroneous, believing mind into the knowing heart space. They are transmuting from the mind into the heart space where the ascension seeding of humanity lies. Through the integration of the seven discourses we are allowing those mantras, intentions and tools to work in a forthright way."

In addition, he said we are being helped by energies coming in from the cosmos (above) as well as from the interior of the earth (below) providing mankind with "an unprecedented amount of universal and cosmic support, energy and love like never before, raising consciousness so you can create communities of peace, love, equality, harmony and balance."

The conversation then turned to a topic that would dominate our discussions in the future, the presidency of Donald Trump. Here is a portion of our dialogue:

> J: Many of us in the spiritual community think of humanity as having progressed a great deal spiritually over the last century or so. Many are confused by the election of Trump who seems to threaten our spiritual progress.
>
> SG: Well, ascension is not always a straight line forward. Let us talk about this divine soul called Trump.
>
> I would like you to begin to think of this individual as making a gift to humanity, a gift from the gods. Begin to see this individual, in order to eliminate and prevent your resistance to this individual— because what you resist persists—as bringing up all the unhealed aspects of humanity and begin to see this individual as a player upon the stage to show the foibles, the follies, the wounds, the defenses of humanity that are coming up for review. Since I was so involved in the creation of the United States of America, we feel you are at a pivotal point in your ascension, an accelerated process to bring up all the things that are preventing America from becoming the light of the world.
>
> J: One of the primary things preventing that mission is all the separation in our culture.

SG: All of that is coming up for review within the individual and the collective. Now you have in the role of your so-called president of the United States, an individual who represents all of the weaknesses of humanity rolled up into one like never before. With the communication systems that you have—cyberspace, the Internet—all of this will be revealed. Then the democratic principles that this nation was founded upon of equality, harmony and balance can come forward, and it can be a test of the true intention of the creation of this nation going forward.

Begin to see this as a play that is being orchestrated by someone like Shakespeare, who we once were. Begin to see this as a human unfolding for you to be able to see day by day. But the mission, as you witness this, is not to go down into it, to be it, to become it, but to observe it and to make another choice different from the ones being made within your political, governmental process. The government, as you well know, represents the people that they govern. You are seeing, by this particular divine soul coming into this particular position, this magnified unlike ever before because of the communication and transportation systems that you have.

J: We have been told by you and other divine realms that there are many hidden forces controlling things behind the scenes that we are not aware of. Because he has not been in government before, might he be a force to challenge some of this controlling power?

SG: He was selected to become this role because the forces believed he would be the most malleable and the most easily controlled. His opponent not so much so. Let's look at this individual for a moment. You have been studying the ego defenses and how they form around the wounds of humanity. You are looking at an individual who is severely wounded in his relationship to dad, with his relationships with his children and with himself, so he has developed ego defenses around him appearing that he is in control, and he knows what is happening. But if you look at his responses through his twitter and cyber communications you will see the inklings of a very wounded little boy crying out in the night, "For God's sake, love me, like me, agree with me."

J: His tweets sound like responses of a school boy.

SG: They are of a wounded little boy saying, daddy, love me, like me, approve of me.

J: So we need to show love towards him?

SG: Beloved students, it is a matter of showing love towards yourself, him and everyone else as a solution to the chaos and the drama that you are in. That does not mean accepting, but *it can mean creating a parallel path to what is taking place in order to create a new paradigm.* It is that intention of the seven discourses and the glossary and the dialogue that we will have with you that that will take place and will affect and support your ascension process.

J: So the material you have given us and our dialogue will help us fashion this parallel path.

SG: That is the reason we are showing up. That is the reason we are making ourselves available. And it is not just with this channel. As we have explained to you, we can be in many locations at the same time. We have selected divine souls throughout the planet to assist in facilitating this.

In reality, you are multi-dimensional beings having parallel lives and experiences beyond your consciousness. Someday, within your ascension process, you will become fully conscious of this as well. If you look at the channel's book, *Divine Discussions*, you will see a dissertation on parallel lives. That will help you begin to understand the complexity and what you are not conscious of.

J: I am committed to understanding my role here.

SG: We wish for you to satisfy your curiosity, to have any concerns that you have or clarifications that you might seek so that we can proceed in a forthright way to amalgamate a document using your gifts and talents to integrate the discourses, glossary and the public and private conversations.

Remember, within your soul plan you have chosen and we have chosen you to be a part of this. So, understand, it is an essential part of the meaning, value and purpose of your being here to be participating in this. We ask you, as we had to make the choice in our own ascension process, if you so choose, to make this endeavor, as you will of your own ascension process, the most responsible, essential and important aspect of being human at this time.

This endeavor, St Germain told me, would be my "opus." "Trust and surrender," he told me. That was all I could do, since I had no clear idea what my "opus" would look like. We agreed to meet next Monday morning and each Monday after for the foreseeable future.

CHAPTER 9:
THE CONVERSATIONS
BEGIN

Our first working discussion began on January 16, 2017, Martin Luther King Day (no coincidence!). St Germain used the occasion to explain Dr. King's spiritual role in our nation, the role of the United States in Earth's spiritual destiny, the problems caused by the imbalance of masculine and feminine energy in our nation and world and Trump's role in creating the chaos which will lead to the restoration of the spiritual mission of the United States.

> Dr. King: The divine soul who you celebrate today, Martin Luther King, is a modern-day prophet who was sent to you to reiterate the Founding Father papers of the United States, to reiterate the founding principles of the Declaration of Independence, the Bill of Rights and many of the documents that the higher realms and I, St Germain, were instrumental in dictating to your Founding Fathers. Listen to his words. You will see they are higher realm inspired, that he has been inspired by a force greater than his blackness, greater than his being an African American preacher. He was able to stand before the people of this nation and in the cloak of the black preacher to

transcend all of that in order for humanity to begin to see the oneness in all of you.

The Ascension Process: In the Ascension Process you are in the process of becoming a nationless world. It was one of the reasons that the archangelic realm of Uriel gifted you with cyberspace and the Internet, so you could free yourself from any nation, economic, political or communication control. You are being given an opportunity to see yourselves as one world, one being and all of you being each other in disguise in order to see the diversification of the oneness, which is the mission of the planet—to learn to love through all of the diversity of creation, the seen and unseen—not only in humanity but in the animal kingdom, the plant, the mineral kingdoms and most of the diversified life forms you haven't even discovered yet.

Trump, chaos and the balancing of the masculine and feminine energies: The foundation of your hatred and prejudice is the imbalance of the masculine and feminine energies, the assertive masculine energy subjugating the receptive feminine energies. That is the foundation of your racial, political, religious and national separations. All of this is coming up in the persona of one that your populists have elected as your president. Within this individual are all the wounds and defenses of humanity. All the people who he has selected to help him govern represent aspects of humanity that need to be cleared and cleansed. Look at these individuals as a mirror of what needs to be healed in yourself. What will be ahead for your country is increased chaos. But this chaos is a preamble to the creation of a new paradigm, which was always the intention of the United States of America—to be the light of the world.

SG: Humanity has chosen to learn what *is* through what is *not*. This is the process that is taking place. Build a parallel paradigm. Do not resist. Do not enter into the fray and the fight, which is what this individual and the forces around him wish to engage because the fight will take the energy away from the need for the creation of a parallel paradigm.

J: What do you mean by a parallel paradigm?

SG: A parallel paradigm involves:

- Love, the foundation of creation, the building block of all there is and the mission to master love on this planet. Through love and a loving relationship with self, mirrored out to others, you can create *peace* where there is very little peace upon our planet for millennia.

- Through the love and the peace, you can create *equality,* particularly with the balancing of the masculine and feminine energies, which imbalances are the root of all evil.

- As a result of the equality, you will have more *harmony* and less discord, which will allow a balance of the civilization of nations to move into a We consciousness, a unified field, a oneness consciousness.

St Germain said it was up to me to decide how to work with and integrate the channeled teachings and the new material we were generating. "It is not a matter for us to tell you what to do or how to do it. You have the template there (Seven Discourses and Glossary.) You will bob and weave through it or proceed chronologically or whatever works for you. There may be current events that will build upon the discourses."

Our first conversation set the pattern for those that followed. Each week we discussed the discourses or new teachings, explored current events and St Germain's observations about them. Most of the discussions involved the political situation in the United States, especially how it related to the spiritual mission of the United States as the birthplace of modern democracy. Here are some examples of St Germain's spiritual perspective on events taking place in our nation and world:

- Allow the chaos, the disruption, allow the not feeling good about what is going on to be the motivation to have an uprising of the principle of democracy that was in Martin Luther King and many like this divine soul who are coming forward. There are individuals who are rising to the mission of democracy, who are rising to the challenge fearlessly as the one Martin Luther King did. They come within the balancing of the masculine and the feminine energy. Women's marches are taking place worldwide in over 120 countries. It is the feminine energy rising up and balancing the imbalance of the masculine and feminine coming forward.

- Remember the cosmic law: *what you cause others to experience you will experience yourself.* What this divine soul you call Trump is experiencing is that divine law in place. His presidency will not be seen by the majority of citizens as a legitimate presidency. Not to judge or shame him, but see him as a role, on a mission, to insure the glory of democracy surviving and moving out into the entire world. Trump volunteered for this mission in a higher frequency format before incarnating on Earth. So did many of your dictators and despots throughout the history of your planet. It is the way humanity often chooses to learn, so that there can be a permanent learning and a permanent healing. Do not go into the chaos. See the chaos creating a pathway to creating a new paradigm, the energy of it as the fuel to create the new paradigm. If you go into the chaos it will consume you, and you will become it. Tap into it by trusting and surrendering that what we say is true and we exist. Know that it is readily available to you.

- One of the major reasons for doing and being this particular teaching at this time is for humanity to trust and surrender to the fact that we exist and to know that there are higher realms here to love and support humanity beyond the human mind. That is a major core value of I, St Germain, coming forward at this time and for humanity to know once and for all that I and the ascended mastership realm exist. We are not some illustration in a bible. We are not some esoteric conspiracy theory. We are a force within you that you are in the process of activating and awakening. What is taking place in these United States at this time is an awakening process, and what you are experiencing now is necessary for that to take place.

- This awakening process will lead to a permanent healing as a result of the ascension process. You have been through these many times ad nauseum with incarnational cycles for millennia and eons on this planet. The time-line is running out (Earth has entered the final 2,000 year age of its ascension process in which it is raising its vibration into a higher dimension of light where life on Earth as we know it will end). There are not going to be that many more incarnational cycles for those of you who choose ascension. That is the reason for this to be put into a concise, simplified version that you—through your talents and gifts and your commitment and your responsibility that you have taken—you will take these dialogues, public ones and these private ones, and you will integrate them into these discourses and this glossary as you see fit.

I asked St Germain about the value of the public discussions since few people, except me, tended to ask questions in a public forum; moreover, few people show up. His answer helped me understand that there are vast unseen energetic forces operating that greatly amplify our spiritual work.

"There is an electro-magnetic grid that goes up through the core of the planet into your emotional, mental and physical bodies and connects with energetic vortices and portals throughout the planet. That is an energetic communication network that is ratcheting out, whether you are aware of it or not, independent of how many people show up or how many people you think read or see something. That electro-magnetic grid going up to the surface of the planet is creating an energetic network of conscious and unconscious communication of ascension. In addition, connecting with these energies from *below* are energies from *above*—the archangelic, ascended mastership, the galactic federation and the star realms—which are flooding energy to the vortices and portals throughout the planet to allow what is taking place now to happen."

Our Monday morning discussions took up to two hours. It took approximately 10 hours to transcribe a one-hour discussion. Our discussions sometimes included new teachings. During our second conversation, January 23, St Germain offered Seven Inspirations given to "inspire humanity, particularly the feminine energy, to move forward."

On February 6 we discussed more new teachings from St Germain titled, Teachings to Free Humanity from the Tyrant, which warned how Trump's tyrannical instincts threatened our democracy. (See Part III)

St Germain's teachings illuminated the challenging issues underlying the polarization and political chaos unfolding in the United States. I used many of them in my blog, Joel's Journal, posted on our website, TheAngelnewsnetwork.com, Facebook and various Internet sites.

Within a few weeks I had written blogs about the spiritual significance of the life of Martin Luther King, the rise of the feminine energy to balance the masculine energy in America and the world; St Germain's President's Day message explaining the role of the American presidency in our democracy; the role of the Trump presidency in awakening citizens to participate in our democracy; the Trump/Hitler Connection linking Nazi tyranny to Trump's leadership in America today.

I was beginning to feel overwhelmed. One February morning Phillip showed up with a valentine from St Germain stating: "Beloved student, open your gift. Look into my eyes. Now look into your eyes. They are one. Your teacher and friend, St Germain." The gift was a round locket with a violet cut glass cover. The inside bottom of the locket contained an image of St Germain. The inside of the top was mirrored, so I could look into his eyes and then look into mine and see we were "one." I suddenly felt a heart connection to a divine being I had never experienced before.

In our conversation that day St Germain said, "Whenever you forget, whenever you feel overwhelmed with this endeavor, I ask that you take out this gift, the gift of the violet flame, and look into my eyes, and look into your eyes and know that our DNA and our spiritual DNA are the same, that we are one. That you have chosen to be a messenger of this specific project and allow that to unfold in divine order. If you so choose, do not become overwhelmed with the information that we give you.

"It will organize itself through your talents and gifts without having to try, without having to employ the mental body so much, but allow the heart that knows exactly how to organize what is forthcoming. For all the extemporaneous things that have been given at this time beyond the seven discourses and the glossary are actually what you have asked for to come out into the world. Are you aware of that? For the information, the guidance and the self-empowerment that is involved and revealed in these teachings are what your heart and your mind yearn to bring out into the world to free yourselves from yourselves and the tyranny of the unhealed self. You have the container of myself and yourself. You can carry it in your pocket. You can have it with you, and whenever you forget, whenever you need a reminder, simply look into my eyes."

As our private and public conversations continued—despite St Germain's assurances—I felt increasingly overwhelmed by the sheer volume of teachings and wisdom generated by our discussions. The question persisted: How do I organize all these teachings and wisdom and fashion them into an "adventure" story? Can I do this? Feelings of not good enough nagged at me big time.

St Germain was well aware of the stress I was feeling. I have a binder stuffed with encouraging messages from him, channeled by Phillip, clarifying our mission and his suggestions for organizing the material. They read like a supportive teacher or parent comforting a student or child.

March 3, 2017

Our endeavor will be a narrative not unlike a governmental/political mystery drama unfolding. We shall tie in current events with all the checks and balances of democracy and reveal how the test and awakening is unfolding, how humanity has chosen to wake up, get involved and protect their precious democracy. For democracy is not a spectator sport. It requires the involvement of all of you.

March 13

As you integrate the initial founding energies, you are becoming a "Refounding Father" of this great nation. St. Germain suggested, "Becoming a Refounding Father of the United States of America" as the title for the book.

March 15

Joel to Phillip: Can the idea of becoming a Refounding Father be incorporated in a more appealing title? I suggested some alternative titles including: Rebirthing Democracy in America, Rebirthing of America and The Refounding of America.

> St Germain:
>
> All will unfold with grace and ease at the conclusion of our endeavor. You will come to know this project is about becoming a founding father through the reconnection of the original energies which inspired the founding fathers and created the nation. Through the process of creation, titles will come and go until one lands and germinates.

April 8

The support system for maintaining and sustaining your democracy are the seven discourses, the glossary and our divine dialogues. Your story-telling narrative is to explain what is happening and why and where it is all leading for the American mission and the world.

April 19

Your story telling narrative is to reveal where the concept of democracy originated and its planetary and human purpose, where it has been and is now and why. Of course, share tools of the discourses, dialogues and glossary that allow preservation of democracy for the United States and how that affects the world.

April 22

> Joel to Phillip:

Please get me a statement from St Germain explaining "where the concept of democracy originated and its planetary and human purpose."

St Germain:

The concept of democracy originated from the Star Seed Council of Twelve which conceived planet Earth to be a combined reflection and manifestation of love, peace, equality, harmony and balance, the building blocks of all creation. You have been taught that your home planet is the result of twelve star-systems coming together to bring the "best" of each to this world. Most planets are the reflection of one star-system. All this is a unique planet soul plan preparation for humanity to ascend into being the "master teachers" in this world and beyond by mastering the relationship with self, self being a reflection of all there is.

Without the participation of the mighty ascended master realms and their choosing the American people and the American people choosing as aspects of their united, divine soul plans—with the opportunities for creating a form of government for and by the people for the preservation of their unified union through the evolution and expression of love, peace, equality, harmony and balance, which assures the success of such a government—what you know as the United States of America would not have come to be.

April 25

I expressed my concern to Phillip that Discourse Two about the I Am Presence and the Violet Flame did not seem to be as experiential and empowering as the I Am teachings given by St Germain in 1932 published by the St Germain Press. I worried that we offer no examples of affirmations demonstrating how to engage them in specific ways as do St Germain's teachings from the 1930's.

St Germain:

Dear Beloved Student,

I am aware of your recent puzzlements regarding our endeavor. As always, I am availing myself to all inquiries and needs through our dialogues. That is the basis of the committed process/endeavor.

This narrative adventure story will include the three of us in a new, concise, simplified current version of anything that has preceded this endeavor. We have discussed the macro/micro timeline of creation, the planet and humanity. *What you are currently feeling and expressing is to be included in the endeavor, if you so choose.*

The material already presented—the Discourses, Glossary and Inspirations—include as their basis many spiritual foundations needed at this time that are being dialogued within our lives, current events and past history.

Your personal stories, soul plans and current events are essential aspects of this endeavor, along with the spiritual teachings, which allow this to be experiential. Seeing what is taking place through your eyes will lubricate the storyline.

Through your resonance and discernment, you will include any past teachings as necessary to empower the storyline forward, and we can dialogue further on these teachings. Remember, beloved students, your individual growth and integration of wisdom/ascension energy during this endeavor is key, along with its sharing.

There is no doubt the three of us are committed to this endeavor. Till our next time together.

Your friend and teacher,

St Germain

St Germain was assuring me that the discourses and glossary contained the experiential information I was looking for. So I looked more closely at them and discovered he was right. Not only are the I Am Presence and the Violet Flame taught in the discourses, they also are discussed in messages from both St Germain and Adama and are the subject of some 60 terms in the glossary.

Here are just a few examples of St Germain's definitions and teachings of the I Am Presence and the Violet Flame taken from the discourses and glossary. I am focusing on them because they are important, powerful tools for "managing energy" and transforming our lives. St Germain has observed, "These are the most important understanding that mankind can ever have." Remember, when employing them, they must not only be thought but *felt!*

- The I Am is the full activity of God. It is the mighty presence of God in you in action. When you *say* and *feel* I Am, you release the mighty flow of this energy. Everything in the life experience of humanity can be governed by the I Am Presence.

- The words, I Am, whether felt, thought or spoken, release the power of creation automatically. The most important thing in anyone's life is the love and adoration of your own mighty I Am Presence, so that you are always fortified by it.

- When you say, I Am, you set God in action. When you say, I Am not, you shut the door in the face of this mighty energy. The student must stand guard over his thought and expression, for every time you say, I Am not, I cannot, I have not, you are throttling that great presence within you.

- The Violet Flame is one of the most effective tools for transmuting and healing imbalanced circumstances that currently consume your planet as well as your relationship with self and others. It can transform anything in your lives or on the planet that does not reflect love, equality, harmony and balance.

- The purifying power of the Violet Flame can be achieved by visualizing yourself standing within a column of Violet Flame, flooding from toe to head and extending several feet on either side of your physical body. Hold this for several moments, allowing the purifying effect of God power to fill every atom of your body. This flame balances your emotional and mental bodies, allowing a balanced flow of energy throughout every cell of your body, raising your consciousness.

- And, finally, this affirmation: In the name of the great I Am, I call to beloved St Germain to saturate the world with wave upon wave of violet fire to infuse every particle of life, every man, woman and child on this planet in an auric field of Violet Flame to protect and awaken them. I ask that this action be sustained until perfection is restored. And so be it.

Months later, in September 2017, hurricane Irma tore through the Caribbean, decimating Puerto Rico and other islands, and headed straight towards our home in South Florida. As it approached the south Florida coast, weather forecasters were calling it an "unprecedented" category 5 storm and urged everyone to evacuate. Evacuate to where? Irma's path was projected to go straight up the Florida peninsula, and the main highways were jammed with fleeing residents.

Phillip and I began invoking the Violet Flame to reduce Irma's impact. I committed to "trust and surrender," striding up and down Ft Lauderdale beach invoking the I Am presence and Violet Flame to dissipate the storm.

Then we received this message from St Germain 9/9/17:

"Your applied use of the I Am Presence and Violet Flame tools are reducing the impact of the storm within your area. There will still be impact which is needed to assist in shifting consciousness. The full impact of the storm will go to where it is need most. Please take note of all the unprecedented storms and earthquakes taking place. Humanity is being reminded there are forces in control larger than itself and that planetary ascension can take place with or without humanity. Know that I Am with all of those who choose to be with me."

When Irma hit the southeast coast of Florida it "mysteriously" dissipated into barely a category one storm but did cause extensive damage on a few of Florida's island keys and its west coast.

As I studied the I Am teachings, I realized that for many years I had already been employing two powerful I Am affirmations that Gabriel had given me early in our discussions:

I Am in a perfect state of health and well-being. It is my divine right, and I demand and declare that it is as it is. I Am perfect here and now. Divine love has met, and always will meet, every human need.

I Am making choices every day that enable me to open to the purpose, the fulfillment and the prosperity of my self-expression in my life. Every choice that I make is moving me towards more of who I Am, what I Am and expressing and sharing that with the world.

These powerful affirmations are gifts I didn't realize I already possessed. St Germain was about to reveal priceless gifts from my ancient past that would change my life forever.

CHAPTER 10:
AN INCARNATIONAL
BOMBSHELL

———

As I have observed, St Germain, in his introduction to this book, states, "Their (Phillip and I) ancient mission of bringing truth into the world would once again ignite." I asked St Germain to explain what he meant. His rather abrupt response was, "What does this have to do with the project?"

I had already learned some past incarnational information from the Two Marys who told me of my incarnation at the time of Jesus and another as an advisor to the Pharaoh Akhenaten in ancient Egypt. St Germain later connected Phillip to a combined incarnation as both the pharaoh Akhenaten and Moses. (which I still do not understand). When pressed, St Germain told me in my last incarnation I had been Joseph Reed, chief aide and confidant of George Washington. In light of these revelations, my current rather obscure incarnation (and Phillip's, for that matter) made little sense to me.

Then, some five months into this project on May 18, 2017, St. Germain dropped an incarnational data bomb on us that still stirs me whenever I think about it. The broad outlines of what St Germain says in his message below, of course, applies to all of us, since we all have volunteered to share this human experiment of soul evolution on planet Earth. Here are excerpts from St Germain's message:

Dear beloved students:

Your many Earthly life incarnations are an ever growing and expanding expression of creation, in your case choosing to be a human being. Hu meaning God; thus, human means, God being man.

Within your agreed upon human contract, through your free choice and will, you have chosen to experience being human in every expression that is possible. Throughout your many lifetimes this has expressed itself in constructive and destructive expressions of energy to learn what you needed to learn the way you needed to learn it. **This is what repeated Earth lives are all about—the continuum of lifetimes to learn what you did not achieve in the past lifetime.**

Conquering physical death, as you know, is the last hurdle of humanity to ascend/transcend back into your formless eternal light body. This is what ascended masters have achieved and is also your divine destiny. (This endeavor offers tools and teachings that will assist humanity to achieve this.) You will achieve this by transmuting your dense carbon-based existence back into crystalline light during the final 2000-year ascension of the planet. Each planet eventually must return to the body of light (star) from whence it came. This is the cycle of creation: from light you came, and from light you return.

Let us now briefly review some of your past lives (not all) in order for them to create a foundation for this lifetime, for our joint endeavor and the continuum of you both being light workers and way showers and bringers of truth and light into this world.

You both are aware of the star systems from which you originated as revealed by Archangel Gabriel (Joel from Arcturus, Phillip from Lyria). You represent and are two proxies of the twelve star-systems that seeded this planet.

You both are aware of the last lifetime you had before this one and its connection to the founding fathers, so I shall go further back. (Joel incarnated as Joseph Reed (1741-1785), an aide and confidant to George Washington. Phillip incarnated as Aaron Burr (1756-1836), fought in The Revolutionary War, served as vice president with Thomas Jefferson and shot and killed Alexander Hamilton in a duel.

LEMURIA

You were elder (Phillip) and younger (Joel) sons of Adama, the father of humanity and high priest of Telos, Lemuria. Lemuria is now an Inner-Earth advanced civilization which once occupied a vast continent in the Pacific Ocean before it was destroyed by Atlantis in a nuclear holocaust some 12,000 years ago. The elder son's name was Christos, reflecting soul. The younger son was Virgos, reflecting truth. The Lemurian culture was largely dedicated to the receptive feminine energies. This was one of your first connections with the cosmic Mary energies.

Your many lifetimes have been about activating the Christ Consciousness, the soul in human form, while revealing the truth, even at the expense of your human lives. Adama is called the "Father of Humanity" since he worked directly with the energies of the Council of Twelve Star Systems that seeded the planet with the intention of being a full expression of the love forces of creation: peace, equality, harmony and balance.

You both committed various lifetimes in Lemuria sustaining universal wisdoms. Your two recent sacred journeys to my earthly home of Mt Shasta serving as proxies to humanity were a continuation of the work you began so long ago. (See Coming Home to Lemuria by Phillip Collins.)

ATLANTIS

Atlantis was an advanced eleven-island civilization in the Atlantic Ocean. The culture was dedicated to the assertive masculine energy. It sank some 2,000 years after Lemuria due to its attempt to control what it did not create—the planet. The Atlantean mind thought it could maintain and sustain the gifts that were given it from higher realms. It could not.

You, Joel, (aka Atmos) were a neutronic scientist during the final epoch of Atlantis. You, Phillip, (aka Spartus) were a spiritual priest. You were located on different islands dedicated to your life's work. You were both made aware years in advance by the Council of Creation that the nation was destined to be destroyed because Atlantis would not be allowed to destroy the planet. Planet Earth has a soul mission to become the full human expression of love (greater than Atlantis' mission) that was destined to affect all of creation. Earth's mission would not be destroyed by an egocentric civilization.

As the islands of Atlantis sank under explosions of fire, you both (through a telepathic connection) vowed to join science and spirit together in what would become Egypt. Boarding one of the remaining space ships loaded with many powerful technical abilities, you set your compass to what is now North Africa, far from the exploding Atlantean islands. Once again, you were about to bring truth and light of the human soul into the creation of a new civilization. Crew members included representatives from the star realms that began the planet, the four archangelic forces of Gabriel, Raphael, Michael and Uriel, the Mary energies as well as the Inner Earth representatives.

The Lemurian and Atlantean experiences were all about balancing the receptive feminine and the assertive masculine energies, which is still taking place now. The reason this is essential is because through the balancing of the giving and receiving of these two energies you employ the full united (oneness) forces of creation. ***The imbalance of the masculine and feminine energies is the foundation for all the duality, separation and confrontation in your world today.***

EGYPT

Upon landing in what would become Egypt, you found a primitive cave culture that immediately saw you as gods, since your advanced abilities were beyond anything they had seen. You arrived with a full knowledge and mastery of the science of frequency technology with which you could levitate massive stones and heal incurable diseases.

You quickly began teaching and building as much as possible about what you knew from Atlantis, though much had been lost. But you and your colleagues had enough to literally lay the foundation for what became the golden age of Egypt.

You had several lifetimes during this period, and I shall focus on a few. Be sure and review (Joel) again what you received from the Two Mary's about a lifetime during this era. (The Mary's told me I had been chief advisor to the Pharaoh Akhenaten who had brought the concept of the one God to Egypt. Phillip's spirit, as a walk in, took over the incarnation of Akhenaten, who was failing, so that the pharaoh's mission could be completed. I, as the advisor, not knowing of the spirit exchange, thought the new-found assertiveness and effectiveness of the pharaoh was due to my coaching. LOL.)

Remember, beloved students, your sacred journey to present Egypt (2004) was a further initiation and re-founding of your ancient connection to Egypt and the continuation of the sending of truth and light into the world.

Early in this epoch, beloved student, Joel, you were a loyal scribe and companion to the biblical patriarch called Abraham where you both met with Pharaoh's

*court, made treaties and assisted Moses in plac-
ing the Ten Commandments within the Ark of the
Covenant, thus creating tenets of balance to further
assist the choice in being human and mastering self
and life.*

*Notice your connection with Moses below. Both of
you beloved students were members of the Great
White Brotherhood disseminating through the Christ
Consciousness spiritual teachings to others whose
soul plan included receiving such truth and light.
You are still being and doing this now. Some mem-
bers of this brotherhood include Master Jesus/Lord
Sananda, Mother Mary, Buddha, Kuthumi, Lord
Hilarion, Archangels Michael and Uriel and me, St
Germain. Perhaps you still feel your connection to
many of us!*

*Beloved student Phillip, as has been explained
to you, you were the pharaoh Akhenaten who, in
effect, is one and the same as Moses who received
the Ten Commandments. Akhenaten's soul mission,
with ascended master support, was to bring a single God concept into this world. Serving as proxies
for humanity, which you beloved students have done,
Akhenaten was the way shower for a one concept
God, and Moses, sharing the incarnation, brought
in the Great White Brotherhood energies to integrate
the intention. The resounding truth of this combined
lifetime is that we are all one.*

The next day, May 19, St Germain added the following information relating to my connection with the prophet Abraham:

Since you have a past incarnational connection with the prophet Abraham, the following will further help explain that connection to you and your endeavor.

- *The divine soul called the Prophet Abraham is a universal unifying force of three of the Earth's major religions, remembering that religions were the first governments in this world. In Judaism, he is the founding father of the Covenant, the special relationship between the Jewish people and God. In Christianity, he is the unifying pro- totype of all one God believers (Jews, Christians and Muslims). In Islam, he was the leader of the righteous, seeing the oneness in all religions.*

- *So, in effect, Abraham, as the founding father of religious oneness, laid the foundation for love, peace, equality, harmony and balance, which later became essential components of the creation of democracy and the United State of America.*

The emotional impact of all this information on me was so great I was unable to discuss it with anyone, even Phillip who had received some information about his previous incarnations a few years before.

During our Monday morning session three days later, May 22, St Germain opened with these comments:

The revelation that you have had is about continuum. It is about the lifetimes that you have chosen to have to gain what you need to evolve yourselves into your ascension process. You have been everything there is to be in being human on this planet—male, female, every religion. You have been healers, murderers, saints, husbands, wives, brothers and sisters. You have expressed all the races on this planet, which reflect the twelve-star systems that seeded the planet.

The most important aspect of what we have given you at this time is seeing yourself as worthy enough and good enough and trusting and surrendering that it is your mission to take this endeavor forward, and that you have the tools, the talents, the wisdom and the ability within yourselves to bring this forward rather than it being just another transmission from the 5th dimension, which you have expressed many times within your Angel News Network library.

It is important for you to be with the feelings, to be with the transformation, the transmutation which is taking place within yourself, self being a reflection of all there is. And understanding that healing what is necessary to be healed in this incarnation, which is what is taking place with this endeavor, is the divine solution and gift of this endeavor. That as you heal yourself, serving as proxies for humanity, which you have done before in your sacred journeys to my home upon this planet, this empowers you forward with a desire and the ability to bring this particular endeavor to fruition.

St Germain opened the session to my questions, but I could not speak. I felt too choked up.

St Germain: *Take a breath. You are not who you were taught to be in this lifetime. You selected this lifetime to awaken to who you really are through learning what is through what is not. Now in your eighth decade you've finally opened and received the revelation, the acceptance, the forgiveness and the compassion of who you truly are by understanding the foundation of the lives that you've had, realizing, beloved student, you have had many lifetimes that you may not be aware of. But becoming aware of this specific relationship—being a son of the father of humanity—is, in your vernacular, the medicine and that healing that needed to take place at this time. Do you wish to share anything?*

I still could not speak.

SG: *I have intentionally not begun the project with this information because what is taking place now through the revelations you are experiencing is the impetus that is needed in order for you to bring this to fruition.*

The adventure (story) is humanity finally waking up that they are creation experiencing itself, that they are God being human. Hu means God. Manity means being man. So your name, humanity, is God being man, man being God. This is the truth of who you are. This is the reason why you are here—to wake up to this reality, to wake up to this truth at this time within the evolution of this particular planet and the human species itself.

Do you understand?

J: I do understand. I undoubtedly understand it more clearly after the experiences of this week than I would have.

SG: *You have finally moved what was trapped within your mental body into your heart. Now that it is deposited within your heart DNA, you will from this point on think with your heart, not your mind and bring this forward. You have made the transition, the transmutation, through the Violet Flame. The Violet Flame is the change agent of alchemy and freedom. You have finally freed yourself from your human mind, the trapped ego within it, the wounded ego within it, and moved that into the divine self within the heart, allowing you to think with your heart.*

J: I have to laugh thinking of when I asked you about my past lives and your response, "What does that have to do with the project?" In many ways, it had everything to do with the project.

SG: *But at the time you were not ready to receive what you have received at this time. All of this has been in divine order, for you were ready to ask. We have access to everything, so we work within the confines of being asked. If you have access to everything and you have mastered everything, you have no need to know yourself, myself. But I'm here to teach and support those who ask for what they are ready to need to know. Do you understand?*

J: Well I'm beginning to understand. When I spoke with Adama a few times in our Divine Discussion sessions (with Phillip serving as channel), he would refer to Phillip as his beloved son. He was talking to me and never let on that I was his son also.

SG: *How did that make you feel, left out?*

J: No. I was just learning at that point. I didn't know I was his son, so why would I feel left out? I was just asking questions. When you said, well, I didn't ask, that was a breakthrough for me, that unless you ask, you're probably not going to receive.

SG: *The important thing for you to know is that you were ready to ask and you received.*

J: It sort of amazes me that Adama could resist telling me. I don't think I could have. Maybe if I were in his (5th) dimension I could have. But in this dimension, it would be impossible for me to talk to my son and not tell him I was his father.

SG: *Dear one, when you are the father of humanity, you see all of humanity as your sons and daughters.*

J: Were Phillip and I actual sons of Adama or simply sons of the father of humanity as we all are?

SG: *You were sons in a specific incarnational cycle, actually several cycles within the Lemurian civilization and culture, yes. What is important for you to know is that you are the son of the father of humanity to heal your relationship with the masculine energy with father.*

The basis of most wounds and the defenses around them is the relationship with mom and dad. Your primary wound is with your father, the masculine energy. What is happening now is you have set up a process through this endeavor to once and for all heal the wounded relationship with dad. Do you understand?

Be with your feelings. Those feelings are important. They are the pathway, the way showing from the mind to the heart. See the emotions, the emoted feelings, as the pathway, finally, once and for all, making the transition from the mental body—the erroneous, believing mental body—to the knowing heart. You were never not worthy. You were never not good enough, and your heart has known that all along.

CHAPTER 11:
MESSAGE FROM ADAMA

Within hours of the previous discussion, St Germain shared a dialogue he had with our "past father," Adama. I am including it in its entirety because of the wealth of spiritual information it contains and its relevance to this endeavor. It opens with a statement from St Germain.

Dear Beloved Students,

Since you are both sons of Adama, I am sharing a dialogue with your past father and myself, St Germain.

Much of this conversation revolves around the Violet Flame, which we (Adama and myself) shall connect into our endeavor. As you know, the Violet Flame is the change-agent through alchemy and freedom. (See Part III)

*What we both wish to reiterate is the level and activation of healing that is taking place for you through the process and creation of our endeavor. Both Adama and I work with matters of the **heart** where all your wisdom is stored from past and present lives. Our endeavor is further allowing you to access that wisdom and heal any unworthiness and lack of self-love, being proxies for all humanity.*

As you know, I have been keeper of the Violet Flame for eons. My soul plan has included maintaining and sustaining the Flame of Freedom (the key aspect of democracy and the Violet Flame) by being the guardian of the Aquarian Age. As you know, Jesus was the guardian for the previous Piscean Age.

Of all of the sacred flames, the Violet Flame is one of the most powerful flames of transmutation and freedom. This is why it is being employed in the protection of the United States of America, democracy and the world at this time.

All the discourses and the glossary are filled with the Violet Flame empowerment. In effect, they are uploads of energy. Let me now blend my energy with Adama and proceed:

Greetings Beloved Sons,

I know it has been a revelation for my youngest son, Virgos, that I am your father. Through this endeavor with St Germain and your commitment to the endeavor, this now has become known to you (ask and yea shall receive). You and I shall continue to have our own individual, direct conversations facilitating further healing within yourself and assisting your endeavor. Please allow this communication to be projected toward the endeavor itself.

While the priority of your endeavor is with St Germain, know that an invisible team of ascended masters are supporting the protection of democracy, humanity and the planet. You are not alone.

As you know, the Violet Flame is a mixture of blue and pink vibrations—the blue for empowerment and the pink for love. That is the foundation of your endeavor—love and empowerment—is it not? Energetically, what is taking place is the merging of the divine masculine (blue) with the divine feminine (pink). Isn't that what democracy fully represents and is missing at this time?

The role of the Violet Flame is to create the needed positive change in your democracy and world at this time.

The tools and teachings and storytelling of your endeavor can transmute accumulated amounts of karma and imbalanced energy from past and present incarnations. Once the energy is fully transmuted (healed) you never have to experience what you are experiencing now ever again. Those negative energies will have been, in effect, eliminated and forgiven and forgotten and transmuted into love and empowerment through the distillation of karma (no longer needing to learn this way any further).

This will allow love, peace, equality, harmony and balance to be the "law of the land." This was the original inspiration and intention of the creation of the United States of America. This is what you are assisting in re-founding that nation as a beacon of light for the world.

Our endeavor will allow all the individuals who did not access available information in the past to now choose to do so.

By changing a negative situation in the nation or world to a positive one and absorbing the wisdom this endeavor is intending to share, in effect, you are sending vibrations of love, peace, equality, forgiveness and compassion that create a resolution when received, creating a balance of giving and receiving.

*By having gratitude for what is taking place within current events that may not seem right (i.e. politics in the USA), you can transmute what appears wrong into something far more positive. This is called the "divine solution"—creating a positive outcome for all, learning what **is** through what is **not**.*

Each situation offers a way to learn what you need to learn the way you need to learn it—not by resisting it but by creating a new positive parallel path. Not allowing the old to exist. You will discover your needs by knowing your truth (who you are and why you are here) and by knowing how to set your boundaries.

True transmutation/change allows everyone to be a winner. This is achieved by releasing expectations of the outcome. By insisting on a specific outcome, you may be preventing the better outcome. Instead, try asking for the "perfect divine solution." Allow your higher self and the higher realms (that know the cosmic configuration) to reveal the best outcome.

*By utilizing the tools and teachings within our endeavor, with no personal agenda, wanting the highest good for all through divine will, you will be surprised and delighted at the "miracles" that can manifest in your lives, nation and the world. **This*** *is how love, peace, equality, harmony and balance can be created on Earth!*

The ascended master tools that we are working with within our endeavor contain divine wisdom and consciousness and are aware of the "cosmic view" and know what is best for humanity. There are untold numbers of guardians working with the wisdom being re-founded in our endeavor. Ultimately, creation intends to give you what you want. You are learning how to be and do to achieve it. Our endeavor is a necessary reminder at this time.

Remember, lack of trust and surrender brought about the energetic fall of all previous golden ages—the original fall of consciousness of humanity that has created all the lack and limitation in the world. Instead of continuing to control what you did not create, why not try being in **acceptance and gratitude** *and allow your abundance to come forth?*

With the lack of trust and surrender in the nation and world today, there is little or no trust in the union between spirit and humanity. As a result, most live in fear and doubt and lack and limitation of some kind or another.

A major goal of our endeavor is to bring that trust back into the world. Now is the time, through our endeavor, to apply acceptance and wisdom in order to regain and relearn the energy of trust—in spite of how things appear in the outside now. This is a process of inside out, not outside in.

Currently, you are seeing in the nation and world humanity learning the hard way. Events are transpiring that threaten democracy itself, and Mother Earth has reached a critical point with regard to human abuse. The new world soul plan is not what government, corporate or religious leaders are saying.

The new replacing the old will be a life in complete union with The I AM Presence of the God-power within each individual—knowing you are the creator creating, allowing divine order to be restored.

Our endeavor is assisting in bringing this truth into the world.

As has been taught, the entire imbalance in the nation and the world is a mirror of the consciousness of the people, their non-loving relationship with self. When WE THE PEOPLE raise their consciousness to embrace universal laws of love and peace, you can no longer elect the kind of government you have at present.

Natural cataclysms, "acts of God", are actually nature's way of clearing and cleansing the abuse of the collective consciousness. When humanity understands and accepts this truth, perhaps behavior can change.

Suffice it to say, all that is taking place in your nation and world at present—war, hurricanes, earthquakes, terrorism, etc.—mirror the imbalanced/repressed energy that humanity has repressed within itself. Humanity has not understood or accepted how they are creating—that they are the creator creating all the time. Our endeavor will be a reminder.

Beloved students, you are creating constantly, minute by minute, through your emotions, creating thoughts that create words that create physical action. And the quiet conversation with self is one of the most deadly forces in your world. Creation is like a fax machine. It gives back what you create through your emotions, thoughts, words and physical actions. Our endeavor will be a not so quiet reminder.

Beloved students, creation hears you and honors what you are being and doing. Our endeavor, through the support of the Violet Flame and the I Am Presence, will assist in balancing out past resistance to past life lessons in order to create the life you are divinely intended to have—one of love, peace, equality, harmony and balance.

Our endeavor is intended for you to learn your lessons in a loving, wise manner where you can have the choice to learn with grace and ease. Past resistance to learning through a higher and easier way is what has been creating the lack and limitation in your lives.

We of the higher realms are not allowed to interfere in your life and world unless the call is made from your 3D existence. ***Our endeavor, together, is our response to your call asking us to assist you to flood your world with the Violet Flame, the I AM Presence and our tools and teachings in order to reduce and***

eliminate your nation's and world's pain that has developed into long-term suffering.

The fifth dimensional world that we live in is huge, filled with star beings, angels, Inner Earth beings, ascended masters and much more. We tend the tools and teachings of higher realms for ourselves, the planet and humanity. We offer the energy from our efforts to you now through the endeavor we are doing together now.

It is time, if you so choose, to bring your own personal support to these higher realm teachings and tools for yourself, the planet and humanity. This is a requirement in the fifth dimension, and our endeavor is showing how, what and why through the re-founding of yourself, democracy, the United States of America and the world.

Your father Adama and your teacher and friend St Germain.

These messages from St Germain and our "father" Adama were powerful and transforming.

I wish I could report I now had a better handle on how to organize and fashion the immense amount of material we had generated into an "adventure story", so I could move forward on our "endeavor." St Germain clearly was aware of my dilemma for he soon followed the last message with this:

Greetings beloved students,

So now you are evaluating and feeling the feelings of having made the choice of being chosen. We/I wish to remind you that it has been many incarnational cycles that have allowed you to come to the decision, to the preparation, to the moment of now to say, yes. Yes, I choose to take my talents and gifts, the activation of my soul plan with material that my beloved teacher St Germain has given me through my beloved channel, and I choose to take this information and bring it out into the world, in effect, assisting the higher realms, which is an important activation and aspect of my soul plan.

We ask you, I ask you, to be with the feelings of **overwhelmed** *and begin to transmute the feeling of overwhelmed into joy. To have gratitude for yourself, your higher self, your soul, if you will, for having said to you, I choose this task.*

Beloved student, the same activation took place with many of the great messengers throughout humanity—be they Confucius, be they Buddha, be they Christ, be they Mother Mary, be they myself. It is all a choice that we have all made to finally accept with compassion to be in service. First, to be in service to the loving self and then to be in service to your world and in the universe and the multi-verse and beyond and beyond and beyond. That is the process, the personal, the planetary, the universal process we are all involved in.

So be with this, and fill your heart with gratitude for the choice that you have chosen, for, remember, you asked for this. You chose this. This was not put upon you as any form of punishment. It was put upon you as a blessing. I ask that you be with this blessing.

I ask that you be with this choice. I ask that you remember and know, all is in divine order.

CHAPTER 12:
AMERICA AND THE
CREATION STORY

By early 2018, a full year after our project had begun, I had filled three binders with fascinating conversations with St Germain (which we intend to publish by 2020 as Divine Dialogues with St Germain), using current events as a jumping off point to explore the vast subject of spirit.

So much for simple and brief.

St Germain observed that we had created "one of the largest assimilations of information from the frequency of St Germain that has ever existed." I was truly thrilled; yet, I still had the nagging sense that we had not fully satisfied one of the key objectives of our endeavor, which St Germain said was "to make sense of creation and reality."

On February 10, 2018 I asked St Germain to supply more information so that we may seamlessly explain and link key elements of the creation story beginning with:

1. No thing which is actually energy and the expression of that energy, which is consciousness, and from consciousness

2. Came the decision to create various worlds, leading to the inspiration to

3. Create this galaxy and solar system and the

4. Creation and seeding of planet Earth and the life forms on it by twelve-star systems, leading eventually to

5. The creation of the USA as a vehicle for We consciousness through democracy, which reflects the soul plan of the planet and humanity itself.

I suggested we could link the above ideas to tell a remarkable adventure story, yet keep it short, clear and uncomplicated.

Later that day, St Germain responded:

> *Much of what you asked will be asked of you to determine what you have assimilated during our many dialogues and materials sent to you. Remember, your personal process within this endeavor is vital. It is your process that is empowering this endeavor whether you know it or not. So take each question you are asking and be prepared to answer the best you can yourself, and we shall enter into a dialogue through that process.*
>
> *So the three essential meanings in this endeavor are (1) The Refounding of America, (2) the second coming of the soul of humanity and (3) your personal process through this all. Stop searching for the adventure story.* **The adventure story is your awakening in your micro/macro relationship to the awakening of the nation and the world.**

That night I wrote answers to my own questions and shared them the next morning with Phillip before our session with St Germain.

St Germain obviously was listening because he opened our discussion with, "That is exactly what I am speaking of. Well done."

I expanded what I wrote into my blog posted February 12, 2018 titled, America and the Creation Story. (Synchronicity: Lincoln's birthday!)

Here is my attempt to "make sense of creation and reality" drawing on the wisdom of Archangel Gabriel, The Two Marys and St Germain:

AMERICA AND THE CREATION STORY

All of creation is a vehicle for God expressing and experiencing itself so that it may know itself as God. All that is necessary for God to know itself is for each *part* of God to know itself. That is what all of God's creations are doing, including mankind here on Earth.

Humanity is involved in an experiential process of discovering its divinity through an ascension process, a process of rising awareness of its divinity. More specifically, humanity is attending a "Loveversity" called planet Earth, learning to be master teachers so that we may teach and manifest love throughout the Universe. We humans on Earth are in a final 2000-year spiritual age—which began in the year 2012—in which this mastership may be achieved.

This great creation story began with No thing, which is simply energy. Consciousness is energy in awareness of itself. Out of that consciousness came the decision to create various worlds, each of which would engage in an ascension process of moving from a limited consciousness of who they are to the full consciousness of knowing they are God (love). This is the process of God experiencing itself so that it may know itself—a process of ascending consciousness.

In time, consciousness created this galaxy, solar system and planet. Planet Earth was designed to be the ultimate experiment in the universe because it was seeded by twelve star-systems instead of the usual one. That seeding created the huge ascension challenge in which human beings would work through the diversity represented by twelve-star systems to discover the truth that we are all individual expressions of the one creator; therefore, we are all one.

Earth, in effect, offers the rigorous curriculum needed to prepare humanity for the enormous challenge and privilege of being master teachers of love and oneness to the universe. This is the contract we human beings have made.

Mankind, in its growth and development, has gone through many golden ages, each with the guidance of the divine realms: Atlantis, Lemuria, Egypt, Greece, Aztec, Incan etc. Each collapsed when their populations disconnected from the higher realms and tried to go their own way.

It was always the intention of the higher realms that We consciousness take root and thrive on planet Earth, as the necessary path to humanity's mastery and divinity. There were many attempts during the various golden ages to seed We consciousness, but they all expired with their civilizations. In the last millennium, beginnings of We consciousness gradually found expression in some writings of western philosophers and in legal documents such as the Magna Charta.

However, We consciousness and the foundations of democracy took root in a more powerful way through the inspiration of the higher realms in the English colonies, which became the United States of America. The Founding Fathers of America and the founding papers they produced, including the Federalist Papers, the Declaration of Independence and the Constitution, were all inspired by St Germain and the Ascended Masters.

That is why St Germain tells us, "America is the hope of humanity. It is the way-shower for the rest of the world. The destiny of America reflects the oneness destiny of the world."

But, in many ways, America, as a model of We consciousness and democracy, has lost its way. Our democracy is now dominated by huge global concentrations of corporate wealth and power, so that our government is more focused on the needs and desires of the powerful few rather than those of average citizens. This is another example of humanity learning what *is* (successful) through what is *not*.

The frustration of citizens contributed to the election of Donald Trump, an authoritarian who, St Germain says, threatens our democratic institutions and our democracy.

But, St Germain also assures, Trump is really serving as a wake-up call to the citizens of America who have taken our democracy and freedoms for granted, as half don't even bother to vote. It is this failure to take responsibility for our democracy, he says, that has put an autocrat like Trump in power and our freedoms and democracy at risk.

St Germain sees signs of an awakening in the large demonstrations protesting the Trump presidency and policies, especially women. "These people who feel this passion within themselves will run for office or support those whose truth is the same as their own."

These demonstrations, he tells us, reflect the same energy that inspired our founding fathers and those who fought for America's independence. This energy is now inspiring a new generation of Americans to Refound America, to re-establish the We consciousness that inspired the creation of our country.

This Refounding movement will be led by the feminine energy and America's youth, whose DNA, St Germain says, has been programmed to begin correcting the imbalance of the masculine and feminine energies that has existed for millennia. This imbalance has caused war, destruction, confrontation and much of the misery of the human race.

The Refounding of America, St Germain says, represents the Second Coming of the soul plan of the planet and of humanity itself. That is why he calls America the "the way shower for the rest of the world."

Meanwhile, all is in divine order as we, like the rest of creation, continue the divine process of discovering, experiencing and knowing ourselves.

CHAPTER 13: TRANSFORMING OVERWHELM INTO WOW!

At the beginning of this book I included my communications with several higher realm spiritual entities—i.e. Archangels Gabriel and Michael, the Two Marys—that preceded this project because they laid a spiritual foundation for this work and offered insights into my own spiritual growth and evolution. In one of them, Merlin (aka St Germain) stated, "We decided to be part of this glorious and grand experiment called Earth life, called physical experience, whereby an *intergalactic movement begins.*"

I asked St Germain to explain what Merlin meant by an "intergalactic movement begins."

He replied:

> "As has been explained to you, your human species on planet Earth is one of the densest frequencies in your solar system. You are surrounded by more advanced civilizations that went through an ascension process not unlike what you are experiencing now.
>
> "Your contribution to creation is to heal your density (raise our consciousness and vibrations), which affects the ascension process of other worlds no

matter where others in your galaxy may be within their process. This is the unified field of oneness. That is what is meant by 'intergalactic movement'. After many eons of expansion (Big Bang) the universe is beginning to contract upon itself, creating what you call oneness."

St Germain said that the clearing and cleansing currently going on in our lives and world was helping to heal our density and create that oneness in humanity, the micro reflecting the macro.

I asked St Germain to more specifically define the role we humans were playing in the intergalactic movement and what creation is seeking to achieve by this movement. (Sorry if I appear a little dense.)

My query elicited this patient response:

"Beloved student, be with what has been sent, and once fully absorbed your questions will be answered. Go back to the beginning of the endeavor. Why has all this transpired? Therein lies your further answers."

I replied:

"Why has all this transpired? To understand and to learn to love who we are and why we are here, so that we may heal the self, which is a reflection of all that is and is essential to moving from the dense Me consciousness of the third dimension to the higher We consciousness of the fifth dimension and above. Because of the unified field of oneness, as we raise our consciousness/density, we raise the consciousness/density of all other worlds, and that is the intergalactic movement Merlin referred to. This is driven by the powerful intention of all creation to unite once again as Source."

St Germain responded:

> "You have answered your own questions. This is THE adventure story: Your self-empowerment through self-love. It is your destiny and destination to one day not to need others to answer your questions because the answers have always been inside you. You are simply mastering how to access them now.
>
> "I promised this would be more than your mere transcriptions of higher realm material. I promised it would be a *full blossoming of you*. And I intend to keep that promise, dear student, in ways you may or may not fully understand or appreciate at present. But this, too, will change."

Despite St Germain's many encouragements, I still felt overwhelmed by the growing volume of information we were generating in our conversations as well as with Phillip's new writings, which had grown to some twenty chapters on what a Refounded America might look like in such areas as education, health, business, etc. (See Part II) We also had begun a program of podcasts in which I was interviewing St Germain about current events.

Clearly, St Germain heard the concerns I voiced at Phillip's pre-birthday luncheon on August 15 because he responded with this message that afternoon:

> Dear Beloved Students:
>
> "You are confusing yourselves and setting unnecessary pressures on yourselves. Let us transmute your overwhelm into wow. Set everything aside, all

that has preceded this support, and now simply follow your hearts and resonance with the next step. Breathe! This is to be simple and joyful.

"Your discussions today at the channel's birth celebration is a simple way to begin: *Our conversations, your blogs and what will come from your radio show (podcasts).*

"The channel is re-writing the 3D applications that come from 5D wisdoms. (Part II) You can factor other elements into this.

"Keep this simple and joyful, creating self-empowerment, not doubt or unworthiness. Allow this to unfold naturally, surrendering to not knowing and releasing expectations of results. Through your beingness allow your discerned doingness to just happen. All the elements needed for this endeavor exist now. Allow them to naturally fall into place."

I responded:

"To me the adventure story is the role Earth is playing in the creation story, the role of the United States in that story and the roles Phillip and I have played in both stories—bringing We consciousness to mankind in a myriad of cultures, including biblical ones. All this seems to make sense of creation and reality, as we understand it, and our roles in it. That's it, isn't it? "

St Germain: "Yes, beloved student, that is it! Now simply allow it to unfold!"

Of course! Since our project began I had transcribed hundreds of pages of discussions with St Germain, which, along with St Germain's teachings channeled through Phillip, constitute what St Germain calls the "largest assimilation of information from the frequency of St Germain that has ever existed."

Plus, I have written many blogs (Theangelnewsnetwork.com) focusing on the spiritual awakening sweeping our country, which is laying the foundation for the Refounding of America to be the "light of the world." And Phillip and I have written our own stories (Parts I and II). Together they capture the "adventure story".

After agonizing about how to write the story, I suddenly realized we had already written it.

St Germain was right: "All the elements needed for this endeavor exist now." We just need to "allow them to naturally fall into place."

He did it! St Germain transmuted my "overwhelm into wow."

Wow!

I confess this last wow reflects my relief that our project has suddenly and unexpectedly come together—and I no longer feel overwhelmed. Overwhelm has been replaced by joy for the wisdom St Germain is bringing to our nation and world and for the healing this project has given me.

It has been a revelation to learn what serving as a proxy for mankind truly means:

My story of awakening is mankind's story.

St Germain: "The adventure story is humanity finally waking up that they are creation experiencing itself, that they are God being human. This is the truth of who you are. This is the reason you are here—to wake up to this reality, to wake up to this truth at this time within the evolution of this planet and the human species itself."

I feel humbled to realize that St Germain is using our book, *The Refounding of America*, to awaken humanity to our divinity, so that we may move into our final Golden Age on planet Earth.

With a full heart I now welcome you to Part II where my cosmic brother, Phillip, aka Christos, picks up the story...

THE REFOUNDING OF AMERICA

PART II

Phillip Elton Collins

CHAPTER 14:
PHILLIP'S STORY

My twin brother, William Ogden, and I, Phillip Elton Collins, were born in southeastern Georgia, near the secret meeting place of the Illuminati, August 16, 1945, one week after an atomic explosion brought an end to World War II.

It was a challenging birth since my 90-pound mother, Joyce Strickland Collins, needed a caesarian section, a risky procedure at the time, to bring her nine and ten-pound boys into the world. Dad bribed medical officials to acquire the necessary medical equipment. We were named after two family men who had helped our father, Robert Eldridge, survive being an orphan in rural Alabama. (Reference: MANIFESTING MEANINGFUL MOMENTS, A Mix of Soulful Insights & Wondrous Wisdom).

Two male twins could not be more different than Phil and Bill, whose names sounded alike, but that was where the similarity ended. Bill was very physical, while Phil was intellectual and spiritual. Later, I came to understand our mission was to honor each other's differences. Meanwhile, older brother Robert Jr. resented two younger brothers becoming the focus of the family. Now, all my immediate family have transitioned from this frequency. As the last one standing, I have gained a greater understanding of my purpose in being here. My intention is that part two of this book reveal that purpose.

Before I was five years old, I was already following my own unique pathway by connecting with fairies and Earth beings in our garden flower beds. I shared my ability to see what others could not with no one. My father's grandmother was a back-woods Alabama healer and herbalist, and I was gradually reflecting the nonconformity of past generations. However, I chose not to emulate past male family members who were grand wizards in the KKK and Masonic orders. Mom's Dad, my grandfather, was head of the cotton exchange in Savannah and also ran the railroad. In addition to the 12 children he had with my mother's mother, my grandmother, he fathered twice as many more children with other women.

Dad's father, who died when he was six, was the first person in southern Alabama to gain a master's degree. He became principal of the local school. Back then, the achievers in the Collins family were men. But I remained forever influenced by one strong female Collins ancestor, my healing-practitioner great grandmother. As I sat by her sick bed, she looked into my six-year-old eyes, took my hand and told me, "You are the chosen one. You got what I got." I would listen for hours to her stories and her nature-based philosophy which stressed the divine order of the universe.

My father overcame being an orphan to become a very successful businessman, pioneering many food-processing techniques that built empires. My mother's beauty and cosmic consciousness helped her transcend her modest upbringing. She was always my champion and defender when I appeared different.

Since my father had no role model during his formative years, his idea of being a father was being a great provider, and that he did very well. But it was mother's affection, humor, grace, style and powerful feminine strength that I would mirror. These qualities would allow me to reconnect with Dad after Mom's transition from this world and become his champion and defender in his elder years. I never resonated with his traditional male dominated perspective of attempting to control people and circumstances through might and right.

My mother and great grandmother were exceptions to the male-dominated society into which I was born. Their influence nurtured what would later blossom into a passionate desire to fight discrimination wherever it lurked. I was preparing to commit to endeavors that would benefit all humanity by reminding us who we really are, knowing the Source of our pain and separation and learning how we can heal ourselves. I instinctively knew the answers would not come from a human mind that had created the problem. I would need to master how to connect with the higher realms to gain the solutions. I had no idea how simple and joyful that would be.

I would come to understand, as the higher realms have taught, that the imbalance of the masculine and the feminine in our world was the root of all our gender, racial, religious confrontation and conflict. There is a cosmic reason for these two forces in our lives, and like the universe itself, they must be in balance. By being "two-spirited" myself, I would dedicate myself to understanding what had caused this imbalance and how to balance it.

Years later, I would study metaphysics, building on my childhood connection between human beings and the forces above and beings of other dimensions.

Eventually, my studies took me to the ancient mystery schools of energy and healing, which led to sacred journeys to Egypt, Brazil, Mt Shasta and the standing stones of England, while maintaining a personal process of a deep examination of myself. Only through healing myself could I better assist others in doing the same. Crawling through the worm hole of self-examination, I came out the other end as a light ascension Reiki therapist, acupuncturist, and homeopathic practitioner. I developed a healing arts practice and later founded a Modern Day Mystery School and taught others what I had learned myself.

Unbeknownst to me, I was now ready to become a channel of higher realms. "We have been knocking on your door for many lifetimes, but there has been no answer from you. Now we shall crash through that door and ask you, are you ready to become a messenger of the Archangel realm of Uriel?" This booming voice came through my friend, colleague and channel Jeff. I had never heard of Archangel Uriel. "We shall give you fifty days to decide and shall be back to you then," this voice proclaimed. My heart began racing, and I was suddenly filled with joy. Even though I wanted to learn who and what this voice was, I knew my answer was a resounding yes!

It is important to explain I am not a psychic medium who connects with spirits in the astral realm (the fourth dimension). The astral realm is a disembodied reflection of this world filled with mischief and possesses no universal wisdom. The higher dimensions I connect with—the fifth dimension and above, often referred to as divine realms—teach truths to set us free from our Earthly journey in order to assist us in evolving/ascending to a higher frequency of consciousness, which is our destiny. The higher beings whom I channel are not going to connect you with a departed loved one or predict the future or tell you what to do. That would encroach on your freedom of will and choice. What I do connect with are higher realms (archangels, ascended masters, etc.) that will teach you the tools for you to make your own self-empowered decision for your highest good.

During my Florida college and young adult days in New York City in the 1960's and 1970's, America vibrated with rebellion, sexual expression and self-empowerment, and I joyfully participated. I often felt reborn in the epicenter of a new reality. I was determined to try to fit in, but I knew I was looking from the outside in. I did not know the term at the time but I was becoming "multi-dimensional." I was in two frequencies/realms at the same time: the one of emotions, thoughts and physicality and another that transcended time and space and being human.

This ability allowed me to develop and exhibit an innate compassion and respect for human life, which would eventually become the hallmark of becoming a metaphysician and permit me to bridge these two realities while appearing normal. I was creating what I called a "new normal," since I knew what I was experiencing was the destiny of everyone. It was my task to be a way shower into this new normal.

By accepting my multi-dimensional self, I was gaining an appreciation for this gift I had been given. What would I be and do with it? I knew it would involve improving the lives of others.

CHAPTER 15:
WAKING UP

———

Much of my education in metaphysics came from the teachings and messages from higher realms. Using them has made my life much easier and enjoyable. As this book is demonstrating, all we need to know is available to us now in our hearts.

I have gradually come to understand that many of the rules and norms of most organizations—government, corporations, religious and educational institutions—too often are created and managed to serve the interests of the few who control these organizations. Rather than feeding the souls and serving the interests of all who contribute to the organization, management more often tries to force members and employees to follow their rules and restrict their freedom to creatively think for themselves.

Most educational institutions do the same thing—too often stifling rather than stimulating the spirits, emotions and minds of their students. They expect us to accept what is put in front of us, memorize and recite it back even when it contradicts our truth. Consequently, many of us spend much of our lives overcoming the limitations of our education, work experience and religious teachings.

The duality, separation and conflict we impose upon ourselves and each other is caused by the unhealed relationship with self, which gets mirrored out into the world. Our world leaders are often wounded little boys and girls who do not have the tools to heal themselves so that they may be conscious, compassionate leaders. This unhealed aspect of humanity has created divisive systems that categorize everything outside their group as the separate "other."

Throughout history authoritarian systems have been created to keep power in the hands of the few to control the many. These systems brain-wash people into a "you vs me" consciousness, which is now threatening the survival of mankind and the planet.

Having been perceived as different as a "two-spirited" male and as a channel of higher realms, I have been ostracized at times by family as well as by those who felt threatened or challenged by who I am and what I have brought into this world. These experiences have shaped who I am now, a conscious being in service to higher realms for the highest good of all.

Old paradigms that dictated cultural norms are now being radically changed with the guidance from higher realms, though the old systems are fighting tooth and nail to hold on to their power. Most institutions controlling our governments and world are dominated by the masculine, directional consciousness. As the women and youth of the world replace this old guard with their new consciousness, they will activate needed change, bringing greater balancing levels of equality, harmony and balance into the world.

In spite of how things may appear, the higher realms tell us, world conditions are the best they have ever been, although, obviously, there is much room for improvement.

As a young student I had trouble adapting to the conformity imposed upon me. In fact, I was expelled from my first college, a conservative religious institution. I knew my innate curiosity was being drummed out of me as my teachers and the administration demanded I conform to their rigid systems and ideals. Prior to this experience I had been a straight A student, but I could not conform anymore. Being thrown out of there was my rocket to a new reality beyond anything an educational institution could offer. My truth and what I needed to learn were inside of me. I simply needed to learn how to access it. I was beginning to expand beyond an imposed cultural view of reality.

I now know that, eventually, we need to move beyond the restrictions of a formal education, corporate job or religion and begin to think with our hearts, if we are to grow beyond the limitations of our culture. No person, organization or culture should restrict another's freedom of expression as long as it intends and causes no harm. It is through freedom of expression that we become conscious cosmic citizen creating balance and harmony throughout the universe. The universe then will support our intentions as we become one with all that is.

CHAPTER 16:
BREAKING FREE

Having achieved considerable success in advertising and commercial film production, I decided to break free of organizational constraints. I became a healing arts therapist using energetic wisdoms and modalities that are not generally accepted in standard medical practice. I soon realized that I, and many like me, are forging new realities that are contributing to human advancement and evolution.

Now, we—today's radicals—must take care not to become the new "establishment," trying to discourage change and innovations brought on by new generations.

This era of competition and greed threatens to destroy our planet and humanity. Rather than oppose this behavior (what we resist persists) we, the spiritual outlaws, are creating new ways to circumvent the establishment and honor the individual by creating a new paradigm of love, equality, harmony and balance. Spiritual training and guidance from higher realms are helping humanity heal the wounds of separation and create a world of healed oneness.

Many are becoming aware of and connecting with the higher realms. Nevertheless, few of us realize that the huge technological advances of the past have been gifted to us from the higher realms (i.e. electricity, radio, television, cell phones, computers, the Internet.)

We are getting a peek at the new life-changing technologies the higher realms will be gifting us as we become ready for them. (See Part III, WONDERS TO COME). We may think the wondrous inventions of the past and present were created by individuals, but, in reality, they were *received* by those individuals from higher realms to help us evolve as a human species.

One thing we do know. If mankind will prepare for it, the best is yet to come. This book contains the wisdom to make it happen.

CHAPTER 17:
THE SEEN AND UNSEEN

I have always believed that the universe works through a perfectly balanced operating system. I attended every religious ceremony available to me in my formative years and sensed the secrets of that operating system were not to be found there. But there were teachings in those religions that seemed right to me. "Love one another" was one of them, which I rarely saw practiced.

I became increasingly aware of the relationship between this earthly world and higher realms, and I intuited there was some grand plan to it all. I sensed we were living at the dawn of a new era–what I later came to know as the ascension (rising consciousness) of the planet and humanity into a final golden age of unity and oneness.

Years later, when I was working with Star Wars' George Lucas as director of marketing for ILM Commercials, I did not realize that George's film stories one day would contribute to my rising consciousness of love, equality, harmony and balance. I would come to learn that amazing stories reflecting similar spiritual adventures are happening right here on planet Earth. (See: COMING HOME TO LEMURIA). The story of Lemuria within our own planet reveals we do not need to travel to a galaxy far, far away for adventure and spiritual wisdom.

While most of the world believes abundance is found in material things, I was awakening to the truth that non-physical spiritual wisdoms represent true wealth. Wisdom from the higher realms contains a vast, unlimited repository of essential information to set us free from our wounding and informs us of our true heritage as individual expressions of creation. I began to see myself as one link in an eternal chain of human souls connecting back to the origins of our human species, and I began to share my insights and wisdom with others.

I knew in my heart that a vast cosmic intelligence operating within a perfect universe would support my endeavors, as long as I had no intention to harm, and they served the highest good of all. I founded The Modern-Day Mystery School, embarked on sacred journeys and helped found Children of the Awakened Heart followed by The Angel News Network. Together these activities represented hundreds of classes, many web sites, multiple books, countless social media interactions and radio interviews and programs.

Periodically, I would stop to assess my *doing* with my state of *being* in order to determine my next steps. During these periods I would be given new inspirations to bring higher realm wisdoms into our third dimension. I knew I would always be given the energy and guidance I needed to help make the unbelievable believable. In silence, I gained a deeper understanding of metaphysical explanations of human existence. I came to know we are here to master being human, not escape it. Through our mastership we can ascend to higher frequencies of existence.

The spiritual endeavors of my colleagues and I have never been about making money. They are about making sense of reality and helping us all achieve our full potential as spiritual beings having a human experience. Somehow our basic financial needs have always been met. Trance channeling requires the trust and support of others. I could achieve little without my colleagues. Collectively we are disciples dedicated to serving the higher realms and bringing their truth and wisdom to all.

We do not require a human leader. Our instructors are the higher realms (archangelic, ascended masters, etc.) who help us in countless ways to bring their wisdom and guidance to mankind. They have confirmed what I always knew: there is a divine order to everything.

CHAPTER 18:
THE PHYSICAL AND METAPHYSICAL

As I have discussed, the universe is governed by cosmic principles which control physical and metaphysical reality. Quantum physics defines the physical as anything composed of energy. When energy is closely connected with other energy it becomes dense matter. When energy is disassociated it becomes radiation. Quantum physics allows us to measure the shift of energy between these two states.

Metaphysics explains the same energy that composes matter. We just can't measure or experience it with our human senses. Soon we shall be able to measure metaphysical events. Meanwhile, we metaphysicians use our resonance and discernment to monitor shifts in energy. Metaphysical experiences, such as information transmitted between individuals, cannot be measured. Even though we cannot measure these energetic shifts (We will as our consciousness shifts), we have been taught by higher realms that these energy transfers occur.

Life cannot be fully explained without metaphysics, the unseen behind the seen. The truth is, most of life is unseen, and, to complicate things more, we do not know that most of the unseen even exists. Translating metaphysics (not to mention the unseen) into vocabulary and language to explain what we cannot perceive makes all this even more challenging. Nevertheless, we attempt to translate metaphysics into the clearest possible terms, so we may understand and explain life. The higher realms are helping us explain life through the messages that we channels receive, (See DIVINE DISCUSSIONS, Higher Realms Speaking Directly To Us.)

Many believe metaphysics was key to the formulation of Einstein's theories. Einstein's formulas explain that energy and mass are essentially the same. He further theorized that these two fundamental components shift from one state to another in human perception—just as snow and steam can transform into water. When energy forms mass, it slows its vibrations and becomes solid. Energy can also transform into light or radiant energy.

Only a tiny percentage of energetic realities operating throughout the universe can be comprehended by humanity, so there is much in creation we know nothing about. As our consciousness expands, the higher realms tell us, more wisdom will be made available to us. The bottom line is we are so much more than our physical bodies. We humans are metaphysical realities providing evidence of our existence to other metaphysical beings through our dense physical bodies. Our physical bodies, which many believe are all there is, are inhabited by our unseen eternal spirits—souls that can never die.

Metaphysics and higher realms live in the realm of no time or distance—another reason why it is difficult to explain them in human language. These higher realms exist in the dimensions (the fifth dimension and above) that I channel. In effect, I (and others) channel bands of energy/consciousness to which we give names so we can identify them (i.e., Archangel Michael, St Germain, etc.).

Their wisdom comes in as energy, which is then converted into language through the channel's body and voice.

Longer ago than anyone knows, matter, energy, time and space came into being through what is known as creation. The science explaining our universe is called physics. At some point energy began to coalesce into complex structures called atoms which then combined into molecules. The science of atoms, molecules and their interaction is called chemistry. Molecules combined to form large, complex living structures called organisms. This science is called biology. In time, organisms belonging to the species Homo Sapiens (wise man) started to create cultures. Their story is called history. Despite how science explains mankind's history, we only know a small part of the true story.

We metaphysicians know our souls and spirits are eternal. We know that human beings are not living on Earth simply to survive. We are part of a grand divine plan to create love, equality, harmony and balance—reflections of creation itself—on Earth and throughout the universe.

When we realize that we humans are on a spiritual mission, the higher realms tell us, we will be ready to advance to a higher frequency of existence and traverse the universe as teachers of love and unity. This new spiritual age, which began in 2012, will bring the great awakening of this truth; only through equality for all can we rise to this mission.

As equality becomes a reality, we will begin to comprehend the truth of human experience. We human beings are not simply physical bodies with the ability to think and feel. We are divine expressions of the creator gifted with unique talents and gifts to serve creation. The universe would be incomplete without each of us, or we would not be here. That is how important we are.

CHAPTER 19:
THE EMERGING GLOBAL
CONSCIOUSNESS

Once humanity understood that the Earth was round, we realized if we started traveling in one direction we would end up where we began. We saw that our own life cycle from birth to death and the life cycles of all living beings were also a circle, and somehow all these cycles seemed to be connected in a vast cycle of life.

Now that we have seen pictures of Earth taken from space, we see how small our planet truly is and that peoples and cultures we used to think of as "foreign" and living far away are actually more like next-door neighbors. Our economies have become global and dependent on one another, and technologies such as the Internet are integrating our cultures. The idea of the enemy as the "other" is much harder to maintain when we increasingly see the enemy as ourselves. Indeed the "other" is increasingly *becoming* ourselves as intermarriage between races and nationalities continues to escalate. "You are all becoming 'super mutts'," the higher realms have told us.

This emerging global consciousness reflects a more accurate view of life that allows individuals and nations to make decisions beneficial to all humanity; i.e., war does not work, pollution threatens everyone's air, water and climate. As we evolve towards a true global society, let us affirm that the citizens of Earth will quickly move from a consciousness of Me to a consciousness of We and stop harming each other and the planet.

While many, perhaps most, believe we must be stewards protecting the well-being of our planet, many governments and corporations act out hidden agendas that serve their own interests and greed.

The higher realms tell us we are evolving into a nationless world. Obviously, we still have a lot of work to do to heal the consciousness that keeps mankind separated into competing nation states. Each of us has been conditioned to accept this separation through our own personal, cultural and national experiences.

Many of us, especially those who feel spiritually connected to all human beings living on the planet, understand this limited view not only does not serve mankind's destiny, it also is inconsistent with mankind's rising consciousness of unity and oneness. This shift in consciousness is speeding up as technology moves us faster and closer into a more intimate, compassionate relationship with one another.

Some world leaders are still attempting to stir up conflict and division among their own citizens and between countries, appealing to national pride to provoke trade wars and even armed conflict. In the past these have been effective ways of maintaining their personal power. With today's instant communication, it is becoming easier to expose these self-serving tactics.

Has mankind's consciousness been raised enough to thwart these age-old techniques of the powerful? The answer lies within We, the global consciousness of the people.

CHAPTER 20:
A NEW ERA OF SOUL CONSCIOUSNESS

The higher realms tell us we are all diversified versions of one another and creation. We are all individual expressions of the one Source.

Humanity's ultimate mission is to bring the message of love and unity throughout the universe. Preparation for that mission is being fulfilled as mankind enters a new era of soul consciousness, moving Me consciousness into We consciousness.

This grand awakening is upon us. It is redefining what we know and demand of ourselves, each other and our so-called leaders in government, religions and corporations. If old paradigm leaders continue to ignore or dismiss the truth and importance of our souls and spirits in our human experience, they will be replaced by those reflecting the new consciousness of equality, harmony and balance. **Our spiritual awakening is the single greatest factor transforming every aspect of our lives at this time.**

Let us examine some key developments, the higher realms tell us, are shifting and guiding humanity into soul consciousness and a new age of peace, love, equality, harmony and balance.

- Increasingly, our souls and spirits will be considered in all decisions concerning how we live.

- We are learning to *inspire* rather than *motivate* each other. Motivation appeals to Me consciousness, while inspiration relates more to the soul, We consciousness. The old paradigm often motivates through greed; the new paradigm inspires with joy and fulfillment.

- Change is all there is, so we need to continually learn throughout our lives. Learning is a defense against ignorance, which can prevent others from controlling us. We are here to grow and expand; otherwise, our souls wither.

- Sacred homes and workplaces are being created to inspire our human souls. Sacred places of love and respect will transform our lives and allow joyful, fulfilling expressions for everyone.

- Each of us has a soul plan, our purpose in being here. Loving homes and work places can help activate our soul plans.

- We all want to have a healthy balance between our personal lives and work. We're transitioning into a complete integration of the two.

- People want careers that produce joy and fulfillment and inspire their souls, not just work that pays the rent. They want to feel pride and ownership in what they produce and to receive their just rewards.

- Through love, equality, harmony and balance we shall create the lives and world we want.

- It is time for the word, competition, to return to its original meaning—to create together. Our world is filled with competition, which creates separation and conflict in which one wins and one loses. Cooperation creates more success and abundance than competition ever can. Let us compete (create together) something wonderful which can create a win-win for both.

- As you will discover in Part III, wonderful technologies await to help us move into a higher frequency of existence and further connect us all.

- The old paradigm of fear and competition will be replaced with a paradigm of love, truth, meaning, value and purpose that feeds our souls and spirits as well as supplying our material needs.

These developments will be spearheaded by the rise of the feminine energy to balance the masculine energy. The women of the world—in conjunction with the youth of the world, whose DNA, the higher realms tell us, has been programmed to heal the old paradigm of duality and separation—will join forces to free us at last from the duality of the patriarchy.

CHAPTER 21:
THE POWER OF ONE

We metaphysicians are constantly teaching the importance of the relationship with self and how this relationship affects all aspects of our reality.

We are all connected and affected by one another in a unified field of oneness. Everything is created from the same energetic consciousness—love. All is one.

Our emotions create our thoughts which create our reality all the time; therefore, we are the creator creating exactly what we think and feel. Inherent in this concept of oneness is that one person—because each of us is connected to all of us—can make a major difference in our world. For better or worse.

This is especially relevant to the question of leadership. The health of a leader's relationship with him/herself relates to their ability to serve the well-being of their nation and citizens. Leaders who love and value themselves recognize that these are essential ingredients in creating communities that can work together to serve the highest good of their fellow citizens.

By encouraging citizens to respect and value each other, leaders can help create communities of peace, equality, harmony and balance. In such inclusive communities, people are motivated to work together because everyone benefits according to their ability and contribution. No one is excluded because they are considered less worthy than another.

Free societies, democracies, encourage all citizens to contribute their gifts and talents, so leadership is not limited to the elected few. It is through free societies that each divine soul has the greatest opportunity to make a difference in the world.

In effect, free societies allow God, Source, whatever you choose to call the divine, to be fully revealed in the world, through its many expressions: us. That is the reason, the divine realms tell us, they inspired the founding of the United States of America—to provide a place for We consciousness (God consciousness) to begin to be expressed in the world.

The United States of America is the only nation on Earth founded to establish human rights. It was the first nation to guarantee freedom of religion, speech, press and the right to assemble and express grievances so that every soul could fulfill its mission on Earth, unencumbered by limitations established by governments controlled by the powerful few.

The United States was created so that the power of one would not be limited only to the ones who have power.

CHAPTER 22:
LET OUR BEING
MANIFEST OUR DOING

Let our state of *being* (consciousness/awareness) manifest our *doing*.

I confess much of my life I lived the reverse. I placed doing, which often lacked discernment, above being. I now believe that once we know who we are *being* (who we are), we can better direct our *doing* to serve our highest good and the highest good of others. The goal is to *be* our message (through our talents and gifts) the best we can without judgment or shame.

The universal equation (Responsibility = Consequence) can help us decide what to do. When we take responsibility for being citizens of our nation and planet, we create the lives and world we want. When we are not responsible, we usually create consequences not to our liking. This becomes a learning tool to help us make better choices. We see this happening in America today, thus our need to re-found ourselves and our nation.

We each have a divine soul plan which includes our purpose to be here. We are all in the process of waking up to and activating that plan. Through a personal process, a deep examination of self, we can become conscious of our talents and gifts and how they might serve our purpose.

We all have an internal gyro system composed of our resonance (how we feel) and our discernment (how we think) that can help us decide what, where, how and when to be and do. If nothing comes up immediately, surrender to not knowing and allow the possibilities and probabilities of creation to come forth at the proper time.

Be patient, and do not allow your mind to sabotage your next step, which is to connect with your heart—to think with your heart and allow your soul plan to unfold. Right now, you are exactly where you need to be—even if that is a place of not knowing. Know that every problem has a solution. Connect with how you feel about what you intend, realizing that emotions create thoughts that create words that create actions.

We are spiritual beings who chose to be human; no easy task. Remember, the world would be incomplete without each one of us, or we would not be here. Once we know and accept this truth, we can dare to bring our greatness out into the world—perhaps being and doing something greater than we ever thought possible.

We are all waking from a deep sleep and learning that we are the creator creating our lives and world. What a magnificent thing to be—the creator. What will we do with that knowledge?

CHAPTER 23:
CHANGE IS ALL THERE IS
AND IT IS SPEEDING UP

Everyone may not agree that change is all there is, but most people are aware that change appears to be accelerating.

Through breath-taking developments in technology, including cell phones and the Internet, most of the world's population can connect with practically anyone, nearly everywhere, almost instantly.

Time appears to be morphing into the present-now-moment where higher realms reside. In fact, the higher realms tell us, our destiny is for everyone to instantly know everything (like the higher realms.) Lies and deceit will be quickly revealed. What a game changer!

Instant connections are uniting humanity unlike any time in recorded history. This was the intention of the divine realms who gifted humanity with cyberspace technology to free ourselves from ourselves. Our connectedness will create a unified field of positive, loving energy uniting most of the world's population.

Tyrants and dictators will no longer be able to control, kill and abuse their power without being exposed. The people of the world will demand and create instant social, legal, political and economic consequences.

All of this is being driven by the ascension process of the planet, which is bringing about a new spiritual awakening for humanity. Earth's movement into a higher frequency of existence is building a unified field of oneness, uniting people of all faiths, races, sexes and nationalities.

While diversified expressions of our spiritual beingness will continue, we will be choosing not to allow our differences to divide us. Instead, we will honor them as we increasingly see ourselves as diversified versions of one another.

The game-changer here is that the higher realms (ascended masters, archangels, etc.) are assisting us in our ascension/evolutionary process. Remember, these realms helped humanity build all past golden ages. Those ages collapsed when they disconnected from the higher realms. Our reconnection with the higher realms is guiding us back to our divinity from whence we came. When humanity accepts this truth, the experience of being human will become much easier. We will no longer see ourselves as worthless sinners, but as who we really are—creation experiencing itself.

If you consider the possibility that we will one day (perhaps soon) connect with advanced civilizations inside this planet and beyond, you can begin to see the massive spiritual renaissance unfolding. This new spiritual age will affect every aspect of humanity: Our social order, governments, religions, politics, energy and economies.

Our global interconnections are vital in the new world paradigm. A world where killing one another to resolve disputes will no longer be acceptable; a world in which there is enough for all will not allow people to die of hunger; a world depleted through competition will be renewed with cooperation and compassion. Kindness and sharing will be the norm in a world populated with communities of love, equality, harmony and balance. This is not pie in the sky. This is all possible, and it begins with you and me.

The organ that we shall employ to effect permanent change and healing is our *hearts*. Stored within our heart's DNA is all the wisdom we need from past and present lives. We are learning to access that wisdom by thinking with our hearts, as we allow our minds to move back into service to our hearts.

It is time for us to create the lives and world for which our hearts yearn. It is time to create new paradigms in government, politics, religion, medicine, economics, and education. New paradigms are manifesting worldwide through a new kind of spirituality in which no one way to truth is considered the only way, and we recognize that we are each other in disguise.

Remember, we chose to learn this way—to learn what *is* through what is *not*—not as a punishment, but to create a permanent healing and to learn that we are the creator creating all the time. Once we manifest our self-mastery and ascend into a higher state of being, fasten your seat belts, for our expanded missions and service to the universe begin.

Those are the changes we can look forward to. They can't come too fast for me.

CHAPTER 24:
BALANCING THE
MASCULINE AND
FEMININE ENERGIES

The masculine and feminine energies on this planet allow us to fully experience being human. The relationship/balance between the assertive masculine and receptive feminine energies determines the degree to which our world is in or out of balance.

"It is the imbalance of the masculine and the feminine, the masculine attempting to subjugate the feminine, that is creating much of the confrontation, chaos and imbalance in your world," St Germain tells us. "There is a reason for these two energies in creation. It is not just about your genders. It is not just about your sexual activities, and it is not just about reproduction. It is about the forces of creation that come together to create. That is the masculine and the feminine."

Without balancing the masculine and feminine energies we cannot and will not evolve as a human species. Our challenge is to balance these divine energies during the ascension of the planet herself. Humanity has struggled with the imbalance of these fundamental creative forces for eons. It is time to stop the struggle, embrace the balance and our divinity, knowing we are all created through the fusion of these two energies.

As the higher realms have told us, masculine domination over the feminine has been the root cause of bias and hatred and confrontation within this Earthly realm far too long. When we heal this imbalance, we will begin to heal our racial, religious and sexual divisions.

Ironically, we are each male and female at the same time. When we incarnate physically as male, our etheric body is female. When we are physically female, our etheric body is male. We can now surgically transition each physical gender into the other. If we can only remember that we often shift genders between lifetimes, we just might treat each other differently!

Perhaps most shocking is that the masculine can think of and treat the feminine as inferior when it is the feminine that *gives* males life and *creates* their physical form! This becomes a form of self-hatred or self-sabotage when you realize both the masculine and feminine energies reside in us all, and we cannot exist or survive without joining them in balance.

It is the divine plan and destiny of men and woman to join together in love, equality, harmony and balance. When we finally embrace this truth, we will no longer be at war with one another. We then can create the new world of community, harmony, equality and balance Earth was intended to be.

This book contains the wisdom and tools St German has given us to help us achieve our destiny.

CHAPTER 25:
HOW WE ARE AND HOW
WE CAN CHANGE

During the past 200 years, humanity has been relentlessly assaulting planet Earth in the name of economic development and progress.

We have polluted our air, water and soil, our bodies, and we are even altering Earth's climate with potentially disastrous consequences, including killer storms, the submersion of coastal communities throughout the world, and the destruction of the habitats and the massive extinctions of countless plants and animals.

Reversing this impending disaster will require an unprecedented spiritual transformation that begins with learning to love and value ourselves enough to love and value our planet and future generations of mankind.

That is what it will take to refocus our sciences, technology and ethical and cultural standards. The most immediate change must be an immediate massive shift from fossil fuel consumption, closely followed by a significant reduction in military spending (the military industrial complex) which sucks the resources out of all human development programs including government, education, health care, the environment and the arts.

In the following chapters, I will discuss many of the changes and hopeful possibilities that the higher realms tell us are possible if mankind gets its act together, beginning with a new spirituality.

CHAPTER 26: SPIRITUALITY, THE NEW RELIGION

Ever since we humans left the higher realms we have been seeking a way back home, for human life is a divine circle of creation. Our lives on Earth are about learning what we need to learn (about love and unity), the way we need to learn it over many lifetimes. Then, finally, after completing this "curriculum," we transcend being human to reconnect with our eternal spirits to teach love and unity wherever it is needed in the universe.

The "problem" for most humans is that this program of "unity consciousness" is the product of unseen forces that natural sciences not only don't believe but also cannot explain. Even we metaphysicians have difficulty explaining the spiritual purpose of human life on earth (this book's intention).

This dilemma has created an opportunity for some individuals and organizations to attempt to control humanity thorough myths and fictions they created for their own self-serving purposes. Sadly, this often has been done in the name of God through man-made religions. (We will tell you what to do rather than allow you to take responsibility for your own life). These authoritarian traditions are losing their influence on our lives and world today.

Religious leadership and practices are about espousing the dogma or beliefs of an organization or movement; spiritual self-empowerment embraces the god-force within each of us. In this new spiritual era, we are directly connecting with the unseen forces of creation without the need for an intermediary or representative (religion, priest, spiritual leader.)

Today, in this new self-empowering age of human spirituality, conscious individuals (this includes you if you are still reading this book) are realizing that we are the creator creating all the time through our emotions, thoughts and actions. We are individuated (made in the image of) expressions of what we may call God, Creator, Source, All There Is. We are in a constant personal process of re-connecting with this "Source" through a process of inside-out, not outside-in. By choosing to be human, we have taken on a mighty journey that is affecting all creation itself, since we all came from the same oneness energy.

Humanity is transitioning from the idea of religion, which is an outside-in process, to the concept of spirituality which is an awakening from inside-out. Spiritual truth, which is the foundation of many religions (distorted by man for centuries) is now an awakening truth for many individuals in which we think and feel for ourselves. Through a personal spiritual process, we are able to transcend Me consciousness and transition into We consciousness that serves the highest good of all.

Religion is often filled with wisdom, beauty and inspiration. Spirituality can take these elements and transform us without any of the controls and dogma found in religion. We are not here to tell people what to do but to offer guidelines, so each may choose the best path to our divinity through our free will and choice. Divinity is our inevitable destination. How long it takes to get there is up to each one of us through our free will and choice.

Religions were the original governments that told us how to live and find God. Many governments today are modeled after ancient religions. When the United States of America was being created, higher realms inspired the founding fathers to separate church and state in order to keep control with the people. Many governments retain the same controlling influences established in the first religious orders.

The word, religion, means to connect. In this era, we humans are connecting with each other through our resonance (feelings) and discernment (thinking)—the energies of consciousness, Source, God or whatever we choose to call it. (It doesn't care what we call it). Our internal "gyro system", our resonance and discernment, can keep false spiritual leaders/teachers and "worship-the-guru" false prophets away. Run from anyone who tells you that you must come to them to find truth or God. True spiritual teachers do not call themselves "masters" but are intent on re-creating themselves in you and me.

When we surrender to not knowing, all the possibilities and probabilities of creation come forth. It is challenging for the human mind to surrender to not knowing or to realize wisdom can and does come from outside our human minds. The higher realms tell us the human mind, in fact, is a receiver of wisdom from higher realms, not a creator. **All the evolution and progress of humanity has been inspired and guided by the higher realms.**

The word, ecclesia, translates as church and means "gathering of people." It is time to create communities of true love, equality, harmony and balance where we constantly embrace our diversity. It is time to be the message of spiritual wisdom. Are your spiritual leaders being their message or saying one thing (a performance) and doing another?

Peace will manifest in this world when we learn how to heal our relationship with self and require this healing of our leaders who, too often, are wounded little boys and girls. The healing of self comes through a deep examination of self through a personal process supported by universal wisdoms (that are easily accessible). Peace will not come through religious dogma. Some of the most religious places on earth are in perpetual conflict and war. Millions of innocent people have been killed on this planet in the name of God. This insanity must stop!

Religious organizations (many in turmoil over sexual abuse and corruption) can only survive if they transition from behaving as dogmatic authoritarians and, instead, seek to create communities of peace, love, equality, harmony and balance. Attitudes regarding religious and spiritual traditions have varied for a long time. Follow your own resonance and discernment regarding which path you choose. Each of us progresses at our own pace on our life path, and most of us are doing the best we can to make sense of life. Humanity is being asked to celebrate their diversity and to remember we are each other in disguise.

No matter our religious or spiritual beliefs, we are all served best by this ancient wisdom: Love one another.

CHAPTER 27:
HARNESSING HEALTH

Ever since we humans arrived on this planet we have struggled to understand how to keep healthy throughout our lives. We look outside ourselves to discover the cause of dis-ease, not realizing both the cause and cure lie within us.

Humanity is discovering that the keys to health and healing are found in the connection between our emotional, mental, physical and spiritual well-being. We are beginning to understand that how we feel and think affects our life force energy within our physical bodies. When the energy flow is blocked or impeded, dis-ease can occur. (For a deeper discussion of this issue see ACTIVATE YOUR SOUL PLAN! Angel Answers & Actions).

Eastern medicine caught on to the connection between energy and health earlier than the West, but we are catching up despite our broken medical systems. Comprehensive, integrated medicine is the catch phrase for the day in which the seen and unseen aspects of being human are factored into the diagnosis and treatments of health problems, often producing safer, better outcomes for the patient.

For a long time in the West, health has been defined as the absence of dis-ease (without truly understanding the true cause of dis-ease). Now many awakened souls understand that health (wellness) is not just the absence of dis-ease but reflects a healthy balance of emotional, mental and physical well-being. With this new "holistic" paradigm, doctors and healers may integrate these dimensions with traditional knowledge.

To achieve its potential, this new medical paradigm must engage the healing power of the patient by incorporating this principle: Being heard is the beginning of all healing. The problems caused by our broken medical systems today are serving as the catalyst for the needed integration of traditional and holistic medical practices.

The true pandemic today is not cancer, HIV or obesity; it is our emotional and spiritual dis-ease showing up as physical disease. Our pain is a wake-up call announcing, "Please pay attention. Please consider making new choices; the current ones are not working." If we continue to medicate or by-pass the pain without listening and acting on it, we will kill the divine messenger within that can reveal the true cause of what we are experiencing.

While genetics and disease agents (viruses, bacteria, etc.) are important factors in health, more important are the conscious choices we make regarding what we ingest and our lifestyles. The innate divine factors of freedom of will and choice are major players here. Remember, we are the creator creating our lives all the time through our emotions and thoughts. (How often has this been stated in this book!). When we take responsibility for this truth, we create consequences to our liking.

The higher realms have told us growing older does not have to mean the slow deterioration of our physical bodies. Much of that deterioration simply reflects what we have been programmed to believe, think and feel.

Let us demand new, comprehensive, holistic and affordable approaches to health care that are our divine right. But let us also not forget that harnessing our health involves taking charge of our emotions, thoughts, words and actions. This is what taking responsibility for ourselves and our health truly means.

Recently I received this message from a friend I was medically assisting:

> *Phillip, thank you so much for getting my ass moving to really start taking care of myself. You set in motion our community, and so much love comes surging forth. Today I had an energized day after weeks of no energy. Now I am contemplating what I want to do in this new transformed stage. You've helped me to regain a purpose in life. I thank you for that gift.*

When a health care professional receives communication like this, you know you are on the right track!

CHAPTER 28:
OUR EDUCATION NEEDS EDUCATING

You are all here to know who you are and why you are here. This soulful experience needs to be joyful. All you need to know is stored within the DNA of your hearts from past and present life experiences. You are learning to think with your hearts and access all you need to know by allowing teachers to become students, students to become teachers.

St Germain

To be successful, a modern nation must have a healthy, educated population. Yet, for many citizens of the United States, we make health care and education too expensive and too difficult to acquire.

Crippling medical bills are a major cause of bankruptcy and homelessness. Millions of adults and children go without needed medical care because of the high costs.

Thousands of students graduate from degree programs every year with mountains of debt that requires decades to repay. High costs discourage countless students from even considering a higher education, or many drop out of college because the financial challenges are too great.

Although both issues need to be addressed, lets focus here on *education* in America.

How can we help students become full, contributing members of society?

To help students achieve their full potential as individuals and citizens, the higher realms tell us we must feed both their minds **and** their hearts. This requires creating curriculums that not only are practical (i.e. math, languages, civics) but also tap into the student's soul (i.e. what brings them joy, reflects their gifts and talents, what they resonate with) that reflects their unique qualities as a human being.

People tend to be successful working at what they do well and love. That is what our educational systems must give students the opportunity to discover and learn if they are to achieve their full potential as human beings and citizens.

Educational systems reflect the societies that create them. Enlightened educational systems are created by enlightened communities that reflect love, equality harmony and balance—the same qualities it will take to Re-found America.

Creative problem solving needs to be done in these key areas.

- Without expanded, integrated support services, students from impoverished areas find it challenging to succeed academically. They need emotional and financial support.

- Educators need to devise creative, diversified teaching methods to reach all students with diversified social, cultural and economic backgrounds. One format does not fit all.

- Technology offers instant access to an almost unlimited amount of information, which expands the student's ability to explore their interests and potential careers. Students must be given equal opportunity to access this empowering resource provided by the higher realms.

As humanity continues to progress through rapid cultural and technological changes, these questions need to be addressed as we create a new educational paradigm:

- Who should pay the cost of education? Since education is vital to the success of society, should it be declared a right?

- Who determines what is taught and how? What is the role of the marketplace in this decision?

- With the increasing focus on science and technology, what is the value of a liberal arts education in life and the workplace?

- In this era of lifelong learning, how can we make educational opportunities available to those who need them in professional as well as vocational studies?

- How can education prepare students to be responsible members of society, moving them from Me to We consciousness?

- How can society better support those who drop out of school? What kinds of education/training would offer the most value for them and society?

Education is the great equalizer. As society makes it easier for all students to have access to an education, we are more likely to create the communities of equality, harmony and balance needed to Re-found America, the nation the higher realms created to guarantee freedom and justice for all.

Education will then be seen less as a privilege and more as a divine right.

CHAPTER 29:
JUDGING JUSTICE

To know what is "just" requires accessing your res-
onance (how you feel about something) and your
discernment (thinking with your heart). This is your
internal gyro system. Humanity is in the process of
transitioning from a system of punishment to one of
self-empowerment.

St Germain

The higher realms tell us they inspired the creation of the United States of America as a place where freedom and justice for all would take root and spread to the rest of the world.

Nearly 250 years later, we find that we imprison more people than any other nation in the world with a disproportionate percentage of the imprisoned being people of color and minorities.

Clearly, something has gone terribly wrong with our system of justice.

Justice is a vast subject that includes issues of philosophy, law, government, spiritualty and ethics. Tomes have been written from every perspective. To keep it as simple as I can, I will discuss the issue of justice from the perspective of what the higher realms have told us.

First, a quick aside. I am still learning that I cannot judge another without first judging myself. My judgments of others are reflections of how I feel about me. Mirror, mirror on the wall who is the guiltiest of them all? Even more reason to focus on the teachings of the higher realms rather than my own opinions.

We know that justice is more than about laws, courts, lawyers and police; it's about how justice affects us as human beings. Justice, delivered or not delivered, shapes how we feel and think about ourselves and others. Being judged by others evokes old questions of who am I and why am I here? Where do I fit in the pecking order of humanity?

When we see a wrong done, we are programmed to seek justice, to right the wrong. Justice served returns self-empowerment to the wronged and helps us live together in peace, harmony and equality. Our society appears to reflect little of these qualities right now and may be as polarized as it has ever been.

Many minorities do not believe that justice exists for them, that it is for the privileged, the wealthy who can afford to buy it or for those who represent the majority—which stokes anger and confrontation and risks undermining our democracy.

The state of justice in America today is another example of humanity choosing to learn what *is* through what is *not*—learning the meaning of true justice by experiencing injustice. The higher realms intended that the "law of the land" in the United States of America would be love, peace, equality, harmony and balance—fertile ground for justice to thrive.

The U.S. Constitution provides the framework for these conditions to exist, including a system of checks and balances composed of three government branches to check potential abuses of power.

Moreover, the Bill of Rights has stood as a monument for human rights for the world.

Our democracy works if citizens stay informed and vote. Unfortunately, the biggest political party in the United states is the one that does not vote. More than half of the population of eligible voters does not vote, which has created the conditions we are experiencing today. Moreover, few citizens have read or understand our Constitution, the systems of checks and balances inherent in it or even know the rights protected in the first ten amendments.

Thomas Jefferson warned that the survival of our democracy depends on having an informed electorate. We are failing that test.

As those who have read Parts I and III of this volume know, if we choose, we can turn this around to create the peace, love, equality, harmony and balance needed to create a true just society. Here is what the higher realms are telling us:

1. Donald Trump is serving as a wakeup call to all citizens who have taken our democracy for granted and do not vote or participate in our democracy. Many see Trump as a threat to our democracy. Consequently, an unprecedented number of people are registering to vote and more people, especially women, who have never participated in government are running for office for the first time. More democracy leads to more justice.

2. The imbalance of the masculine and feminine energy— the assertive masculine energy subjugating the receptive feminine energy—is the foundation of our racial, political, religious and national hatreds and separations. Women are standing up and saying they have had enough. It is the rising of the feminine energy to

balance the masculine that will restore the equality, harmony and balance necessary for true justice to thrive in our society.

3. We have been gifted by the higher realms with cyberspace and the Internet, so that we may free ourselves from the control of any nation, economic or political system. Freedom is necessary for justice to thrive. The higher realms will continue to empower us with new technologies as we are ready. Are we ready?

4. The United States was created by the higher realms to plant the seeds of We consciousness (the consciousness of justice) on earth. It is the divine mission of the United States to spread We consciousness to the world. We who are seeking to create true justice in America are supported by a vast cosmic support system. We are not alone. But it is our job to create the equality, harmony and balance necessary to create the just society we all seek.

This book, *The Re-founding of America*, contains the tools we need to create the system of justice America was intended to have. What do we choose to do with them?

CHAPTER 30:
MEDIA AS THE MESSAGE

The United States of America was designed to be a "platform for bringing We consciousness and equality, harmony and balance into existence within this planet," St Germain declares in Parts 1 and 3 of this work.

That is why he continually urges us to create *communities* of equality, harmony and balance, so that we may form *governments* of the people, by the people and for the people—governments reflecting We consciousness.

Our media can do a better job of supporting our nation's divine design.

Broadcast and print media have the potential to help bring us together in inclusive communities or drive us apart. Most of us have strong opinions about which specific media fall into which category. Though some media today contribute to the polarization of our culture, nevertheless, the last hundred years has spawned an incredible explosion in the number, diversity and technology of media.

In our country, media have grown from a relatively few magazines (though we had more newspapers) and primitive radios to thousands of publications and sophisticated broadcast media—not to mention a large array of technological devices that give private citizens access to more information than was available to our President only a few decades ago.

Cyberspace and the Internet have freed us from the control of any nation or economic or political system by providing instant connection between most of the human population on the planet.

A brief but important aside here about cyberspace. It is a gift from the higher realms, but not without risks, since—because of our free will and choice—we are free to use it anyway we choose. And there are unhealed forces that are using cyberspace to spread untruths. It is essential that we use our resonance and discernment to discover what is truth and what is not.

Nevertheless, if fast information and communication are fundamental to creating inclusive communities—and they are—they are now in place.

How do we influence media to help bring us together in communities of equality, harmony and balance? In a free, capitalistic society, organizations can only succeed if they attract enough customers to support them. If we wish to have inclusive media organizations, it is in our power to have them by only supporting media which honor that mission.

When you finish this book perhaps you will be motivated to support media that include inclusiveness in their mission.

CHAPTER 31:
WHY THE ARTS?

You are all here to create by bringing your talents and gifts out into the world. What and how you create is something called the ARTS: Awakening Relevant Truth Soulfully, which is achieved through your soul-energy, the unseen aspect of yourself that empowers your physical being.

St Germain

As St Germain tells us, the arts are a vehicle for expressing our soul's creativity. Historians have observed that long after memories of a civilization's commerce and daily affairs have faded or been forgotten, it is its arts that are remembered.

Old paradigms have always been transformed into the new through our creative process. As St Germain suggests, art is the creative tool of the human soul to help humanity advance into higher states of existence, eventually freeing us from the old to create a better new.

Throughout history, the arts have been attacked by those who wish to control the people and/or the artistic expression of art itself. Funding for the arts has been under attack in our country for years. Funding and art programs in schools throughout the country have been cut or eliminated. While national support for theaters, symphony orchestras and opera companies are common in many countries, such support is rare in the United States. Most artistic organizations here struggle to survive.

The United States, as we have noted here many times, was inspired to be a "nursery" for We consciousness on Earth. The arts are a divine expression of We consciousness.

Perhaps, one day this nation will come to appreciate that the arts are a perfect medium to help us fulfill our divine mission.

CHAPTER 32:
GOOD GOVERNANCE

To govern is to know how to use your God-given energy for the highest good of all. Your present governments often reflect old-time religions attempting to control what they did not create. This is impossible.

St Germain

PART 1

Good governance seeks to serve the "highest good for all," says St Germain. The only way that goal can be achieved is for all citizens to have the opportunity to participate equally in their government. By serving *individuals* equally, governments may serve *all* equally.

That is what the United States was divinely created to do. Ours is the first government on Earth founded with the mission to guarantee human rights.

Historically, power and wealth have gravitated to the few in every civilization and culture. It usually remained there for generations because the same wealthy and powerful few also controlled the government to the near exclusion of most citizens.

Those systems of government were called tyranny by the American colonists who revolted and created a government called democracy that included a system of checks and balance designed to distribute rights and power equally.

The new system was flawed, however, because many rights, including the vote, were limited to the few (mostly white male landowners). Gradually many rights, including the vote, have been broadened over the years to be more inclusive.

However, our American democracy is still a work in progress. We currently are seeing our system of checks and balances does not work well when one political party controls the presidency and both houses of congress. If this control lasts long enough, one party can also control appointments to the judiciary, which can undermine the concept of equal justice for all.

(Notice how often I am using the word, control, in this piece. Now consider St Germain's opening comments about control.)

Another method of control, gerrymandering—designing voting districts to guarantee (control) elections results—has become widespread, currently occurring mostly in Republican controlled states. Some of these same states also have been trying to limit access to the ballot (more control) in districts populated by the poor and/or minorities considered likely to vote democratic. Gerrymandering, one should note, historically has been practiced by both political parties.

Unquestionably, the biggest failing in the functioning of our democracy has been the U.S. citizenry itself. As we have noted, more than half of eligible voters do not vote in presidential elections, and nearly two-thirds do not vote in mid-term elections. While average citizens are playing a smaller role in our democracy, wealthy donors and organizations increasingly control our political system and government.

Clearly, our system is not serving the "highest good for all."

As the higher realms have pointed out many times in this book, Responsibility = Consequences. When we don't take responsibility for obtaining what we want and need, we reap consequences not to our liking. Do you like what is going on in our country today? If you're reading this book, your answer likely is, no!

That is why we are writing this book to Re-found America—led by one of the ascended masters who started it all, St Germain—so that we may fulfill America's mission to seed We consciousness on Earth.

All we need to know to Re-found our divinely inspired nation is contained in this divinely inspired book.

PART 2

St Germain's warnings about political control requires a look at the Presidency of Donald Trump.

St Germain encourages us to see Trump as a kind of Shakespearean figure showing us all the weaknesses of humanity that are preventing America from fulfilling its mission as the "light of the world." He warns us not to enter into Trump's lower vibrations by resisting him (what we resist persists) but to create a parallel path of higher vibrations to create a new paradigm reflecting Earth's divine mission.

What lower vibrations is Trump showing us? Instead of bringing us together, he has been separating us by appealing to fear, bigotry, and lies. Instead of seeking common ground and compromise, he attacks adversaries, setting up the dynamic of "I win, you lose." He appears to have little knowledge or regard for the constitution or the rule of law and repeatedly attacks our free press, our legal system and any checks on his authority. His political rallies, unprecedented for a president not campaigning, exude the energy of violence similar to the rallies of Hitler and Mussolini. His is the dark path of low vibrations created by the despots of history who seek only to control.

Conversely, St Germain tells us, the mission of the United States is to create communities of peace, love, equality, harmony and balance—the path of high vibrations.

Yes, we must vote; yes, we must participate in our democracy, including running for office; yes, we must make our voices heard and speak our truth. Is this really enough? When truth, decency and our democracy are under attack, shouldn't we fight back in every way possible?

Yes, St Germain says, but not by wasting our energy by attacking and mirroring the behavior we reject. Fighting the opposition energizes it. When we mirror the energy/behavior of the darkness, we become the darkness. That is why what we resist persists.

Instead, we must create a parallel path of higher vibration, reflecting the love, peace, harmony, equality and balance we wish to create. That is the *hard* thing to do, but it is the *smart* thing to do because when we create a parallel path of higher vibrations, the lower vibrations entrain to the higher vibration. That is how permanent change happens

This has been taught by great spiritual figures such as Buddha and Jesus and has been demonstrated by more contemporary figures such as Lincoln, Gandhi, Mother Theresa, Nelson Mandela, and Martin Luther King.

This is the new paradigm that will revitalize our democracy and help America reclaim our destiny as the "light of the world."

CHAPTER 33:
WHAT'S UP WITH DEATH?

You are mastering the reality that you can never truly die, that you are eternal beings at present choosing to have physical human experiences. You are transitioning/ascending from the physical into the non-physical. This is your destiny, your divine destination.

St Germain

We are beginning to understand the relationship between our imbalances, unhealed ego defenses, our negative thoughts and emotions and our physical deaths. This "discord" within us actually creates our disintegration, which is another name for death.

As we are reminded throughout this book, we are in the process of learning to love self and others and have this love reflect out in all aspects of our lives in order to reclaim our immortal state of being. In effect, mankind is learning to live by the eternal law of love.

God is the essence of this thing called love. And when we learn how to fully integrate this love into our civilization and ourselves, we can and will be released from the cosmic wheel of birth and rebirth. Repeated Earth lives will no longer be necessary, and the imbalances/problems we experience now will disappear. We simply will no longer need to learn the way we have learned in the past (often through what is not).

Rather than learn through lack and limitation, duality, separation and confrontation, we will experience joy and abundance in ever-expanding perfection, which forever manifests within love. Our old selves and death will simply vanish into our new state of being.

When our human wounds, defenses, and discord dissolve, not by so-called death but by constantly raising our consciousness through our I Am presence (our connection to Source), We consciousness will be released into the outer world. We conscious fueled by the I Am energies will usher humanity into its final golden age.

Through We consciousness, every human being can release the limitless God Power of the mighty I Am presence within to build communities of equality, harmony, and balance worldwide—just like the all-powerful ascended masters who once walked this Earth and continue to support us now. This is the cosmic Christ/God Power within us all!

Throughout the universe, We consciousness is the only consciousness that can say I Am. When we choose to say, I Am, we are being and using the divine power of our personal God-power.

St Germain has gifted us with this beautiful teaching about death:

WHAT WE CALL DEATH

Death is feared.
And yet ever so near.
Let us re-train ourselves
Through another view
And review a new view
Of what we call death.

Death is but an opportunity
For rest and re-attunement,
To free us from the out-of-tunement,
Turmoil and imbalances of being Earth-bound,
Long enough to heal enough
To decide if we want another ride
On the physical side.

Perhaps physical format's only reason to be
Is for preparing, perfecting our human body
For another toddy, mixing and blending with its
Spiritual body, once again.

Maybe this reunion with spirit
Is the real reason for human experience,
At all.

When a loved one has passed on
They are actually with their higher body consciousness,
Causing celestial bliss.

If we could only remember
Our body is only a wardrobe,
We wear for a moment,
Until we shed it,
To accept a better opportunity to bed,
A fuller moment.

It is the unknowing of these truths
Which hamper humanity and keep
Us in self-created chains of non-clarity.

We get stuck and refuse
To understand the true cycle of life,
Dragging ourselves into stiff with self-pity,

Breaking down our resistance,
Creating more persistence in the resistance,
And what we resist, persists.

It is the lack of knowing our
True spiritual composition
That keeps us in the position
Of lack and limitation.

Let us celebrate and emulate
The fact that we are eternal beings.
Who can never die,
And when we leave these bodies,
Which we have done thousands of times before,
We shall mourn never more,
Knowing we have gloriously returned home,
To decide what our next roam, ride and home,
Shall be.

(From *Sacred Poetry and Mystical Messages*
received by Phillip Collins from St Germain)

CHAPTER 34:
ST GERMAIN EXPLAINS
IT ALL FOR YOU

Mankind's economic and technological development over the last few hundred years is nothing short of breathtaking.

We have made huge strides in travel, communication, medicine, the sciences, technology, manufacturing and commerce, which have supplied most of us with countless creature comforts. Most people in the world live vastly more comfortable lives than did royalty when America was discovered. We are living healthier, longer lives than any time in recorded history.

But how much have we truly progressed? Along with this progress has come the ability to destroy the planet and all life upon it. In "developing" our world we have ravaged our planet and become the scourge of every life form upon it.

What's more, we do not know the answers to the most basic, fundamental questions about life:

Is there a God? What/who is it/he/she? Who are we? Why are we here? How did Earth go from a molten rock to a planet teeming with life? Where did man come from? What creates life? What happens at death? What is the true history of life on Earth? What is consciousness? Are we alone in the galaxy, the universe? Why is there so much evidence of ancient advanced civilizations, yet history ignores, denies or cannot explain them? How could slaves build the pyramids, the oldest structures on Earth, with stone blocks heavier than modern equipment can lift and then join them in perfect align-ment—not only with each other but also with the stars? Etc., etc.

Sciences and religions offer some answers, but woe to anyone, professional or not, who challenges their belief systems.

Welcome to the Re-founding of America, inspired by St Germain, who is challenging everything you thought you knew about nearly everything.

In Part III, St Germain provides more information about man-kind's earthly journey, tells us of the vast cosmic support system guiding us and offers tools to empower us to become what he is: an ascended master, a human being who has raised his consciousness from the limitations of the third dimension to the unlimited powers of the fifth dimension.

Here is the wisdom to help us fully heal and reinvigorate not only our own lives but also the divine mission of the United States of America to be the "light of the world."

Please now enter Part III, a course in Ascended Mastership from St Germain. Enjoy!

PART III

ST GERMAIN'S SEVEN ASCENSION DISCOURSES

INTRODUCTION

The great Ascended Master, Saint Germain, who has played an essential role in the spiritual evolution of humanity for thousands of years, gave these teachings to us. Saint Germain was a key force in the founding of the United States of America as a sanctuary for freedom and equality.

Ascended Masters are *higher realm divine beings* who were once human and chose to ascend from a dense third dimensional reality into the higher frequency of the fifth dimension, the divine destiny/destination of all humanity. They achieved this by making their ascension the priority of their Earthly lives so that they might transmute from the dualistic Me consciousness (third dimension) into the higher vibrational state of the unified We consciousness (fifth dimension).

These new teachings reveal how we also may ascend from the third to the fifth dimension and achieve our own personal Ascended Mastership.

Since many extensive teachings of Saint Germain already exist (and are widely available through the Internet), St. Germain tells us these discourses offer a "simplified teaching designed to give you a more immediate connection with the frequency you are to become."

A significant body of these discourses focuses on the self-empowering tools of the **I AM Presence** and the **Violet Flame,** which assist humanity in raising our energetic frequency, so we can ascend into a higher frequency of existence. It is the soul plan option for each of us to become Ascended Masters during this new 2,000-year *Age of Aquarius*.

Saint Germain is asking us: "Are you ready to wake up, to be and do the work necessary to receive your Divine Gift of Ascension, to awaken to your true selves and purpose in being here?" He has given us the tools here to accomplish this.

I humbly present these **Seven Discourses**, which I received from St. Germain, for your consideration through your resonance and discernment

Phillip Elton Collins

DISCOURSE #1

WHO I AM AND WHO YOU SHALL BECOME

Beloved Students,

It is essential for you to know and remember that I have been human just like you. Many of the higher realms have never been human. I am proof that you can and will achieve what I have chosen to be and do—to become an Ascended Master. I am the divine way shower, and so are you.

Like you, I have had many incarnations on this planet. Not to overload you with historical information, I shall briefly review some (not all) significant ones. You, too, have had some life times that made a huge difference in the ascension of the planet and humanity.

I was the father of Jesus and the husband of Mary. I was the alchemist and prophet Merlin during the court of King Arthur. I was Christopher Columbus who re-discovered North America. I was Francis Bacon, statesman, philosopher and literary master you know as Shakespeare. My last human life time was the Count Saint Germain where I assisted in the creation of The United States of America (USA) and received my dispensation to ascend. All these incarnations were experienced within a 2,000-year Earth cycle ending during your 19th century.

We of the Ascended Mastership Realms consider this endeavor a simplified, concise teaching of all that has preceded it.

The meaning and value of this outreach is for you to have a more immediate connection/dialogue with the frequency you are destined to become.

This in no way attempts to be a complete teaching from our fifth dimensional realm. *It is our intention that some of your fear, doubt and ignorance regarding us is healed through this interchange.*

Once there is further trust that we truly exist and you fully surrender/receive our love and support, the sooner your ascension process will flow with grace and ease.

It is within your divine soul plan that each of you becomes an Ascended Master. This is your destiny that no one and no thing can take away from you. It has only been through your mental bodies thinking you are not good enough or worthy enough that you have built a resistance to your birthright. What you have been taught about yourself is now being retaught, if you so choose, to make another choice now.

You are a divine spiritual being choosing to have a human experience in order to master the human self so that you may embrace your ascended mastership. The human choice you have made is an essential aspect of creation expressing itself in order to advance creation itself. We of the higher realms honor the choices and challenges you have made for the betterment of ALL THERE IS.

Once you achieve your full ascended state through something called your higher self, I AM Presence and world service, your service to all creation begins. In addition to your I AM Presence, together we shall also be employing the Violet Flame to assist you in achieving your ascended mastership.

Both the I AM Presence and The Violet Flame utilize the cosmic laws and science of frequency and vibration. Mastership is all about mastering the use of energy through frequency and vibration. This allows you to manifest what you intend through focusing your attention. There will be more on these within our dialogue later.

All creation would be incomplete without each and every one of you; otherwise, you would not be here. When you trust, surrender and embrace this truth, your resistance will vanish like the wounds and ego defenses you created to survive being human.

The thing that humanity fears the most is recognizing and embracing your divinity through your I AM Presence that lives within your hearts. For eons, those working on the dark side of humanity have taught you that you are something else in an attempt to control you. And they have done a pretty good job. But what these hidden forces do not realize is they cannot permanently control what they did not create. And they did not create this world or you.

Your emotional and mental bodies have been filled with erroneous belief systems that are not true. There has actually been very little truth in your world. But the truth will set you free, and it is available to you now, if you so choose to receive/accept it. We of the higher realms have gifted you with cyber communication systems to free you from the control of others, even as these are attempting to be controlled now. Use your resonance (how you feel about it) and your discernment (how you think about it) as your internal gyro system to know what to know and bring into your life and world.

Your ascension process is all about raising your vibration/frequency through your awareness/consciousness so you can transmute/transcend/ascend into a higher frequency of existence. The higher realms cannot allow a lower frequency within them. Right now, your present frequency is preventing your ascension. We of the higher realms continue to send you ways and means to heal yourself so we may join as One. Endeavors such as *The Angel News Network* and others are dedicated to sending our support to you while also allowing you to have direct access to us.

We again acknowledge the choices you have made in being human, learning the way you have chosen to learn what you need to master in order to free yourself from yourself. Please know this is the only way there could be a *permanent healing* due to the demise of past golden ages because of your disconnect from higher realms (the human mental body thinking it could be and do it a better way). *The goal is for you to achieve a permanent connection to the higher realms so that together we can be in service to ALL THERE IS.*

As your planet moves into its final 2,000-year cycle of creating the final seventh golden age of returning to light from whence all came, your healing and transformation will come through a personal process that requires you being and doing the work and accepting with compassion, thus forgiving, how you have chosen to learn. ***All the tools you need to master self are available in great detail through this endeavor and others.***

Your ascension process does not have to be as painful as your experiences in the past. It is not a punishment. The universe is built upon love. The pain does not have to continue to be long-term suffering. Right now, if you so choose, you can see this as the grandest journey of all your lifetimes joined with us working together hand and hand, heart to heart. Remember, our DNA is the same, since we walked where you are walking now. We ask that you join us knowing we have been where you are and have made another choice to ascend.

We of the Ascended Realms are committed to supporting you as you transform your world into communities of equality, harmony and balance through a loving relationship with self. When you are ready to meet our commitment and make it the most important priority in your life, our world will become one.

There is actually a co-dependence between our dimensions. As our frequencies join as one, it allows the destiny of humanity and this planet to be further fulfilled: *to become the master teachers of the universe.* This is who you truly are and why you are here. This is the big picture!

For your destiny to take place you need to master self and manifest this final golden age through the application of love (the building block of all). When you have reflected love in all human endeavors, all your beingness will entrain to this highest frequency, and you will transmute into your light bodies and become the Ascended Masters you are destined to be in being human.

As we further embark on this dialogue, let us fill our hearts and eternal souls with the ascension fire that burns within you. I am Saint Germain, your ascended way shower, teacher, brother and friend.

Your Teacher & Friend,

St Germain

DISCOURSE #2

THE I AM PRESENCE & THE VIOLET FLAME

Beloved Students,

The purpose of this discourse and dialogue is to further reveal two essential tools within your ascension process—moving these tools from being an abstraction to becoming integrated, applied knowledge/wisdom.

You are a wise and eternal being, and you have chosen to incarnate in this time and space to assist with the evolution of human consciousness.

Your I AM Presence is your original and permanent connection to your eternal, Divine Higher Self and we Ascended Masters as well. *It is a gift from the gods, an insurance policy that will never expire.* You are born from the I AM, and you will return to it. There is no other way to be. This is creation creating.

What you choose to experience between your I AM and human lifetimes (your sacred journeys) is how you choose to learn what you need to learn through your freedom of choice and will. Within the reality of Oneness, this is how the universe keeps eternally growing and expanding.

There are different frequencies and vibrations (intentions) within each of your lifetimes. The meaning, value, purpose and intention of each lifetime are to learn to *master love, since love is the foundation of all creation.* Everything else is the absence of love. And you have been experiencing a lot of this. You are learning what *is* through what is *not*. This is not the easiest path to wisdom but the one you have chosen in order to effect a permanent healing, so you may achieve your ascension.

Through the ascension process of the planet herself, you are also experiencing your personal human ascension process of moving from *a dense carbon-based reality (frequency) to crystalline/ light formatting*. The human contract for how you have chosen to learn in the past (through duality, separation and conflict) is coming to an end, as you have the choice now to stay connected to your I AM Presence and (fifth dimensional) higher realms supporting your transition/ascension.

You are becoming multidimensional, and the time to bridge the separation between dense matter and higher realms is upon you. You are in the process of embracing your true divine nature and your Oneness with ALL THERE IS. You have been preparing for this ever since you came to this planet from other worlds.

Let us now review some of the wisdoms that are contained within your I AM Presence that you are continuing to master:

- All you have agreed to experience has been a pathway awakening your consciousness (ascension process) to knowing *you came from love, you are love, loved and lovable.*

- There is plenty to be and do here now, but know when your Earth journey is complete your cosmic journey begins as an *ascended being of light.*

- Cosmic and ascension energies are coming into your world and lives like never before, empowering you homeward.

- Universal wisdoms are coming into your consciousness along with how to apply them.

- You are experiencing Oneness/We Consciousness through a healed relationship with self. This is a *transition into the infinite.*

- Joy, bliss and peace are the emotions powering your pathways.

- You are beginning to remember *you are an eternal, formless being of light* having a human experience.

- You are mastering who you are and why you are here.

- Your human self is finding its eternal self.

All spoken here is *stored within the DNA of your heart,* and you are learning to think with your heart, as your believing mind moves into service to your knowing heart.

THE VIOLET FLAME

As many of you know there are several sacred flames, which various Ascended Masters work with. These *flames are bands of energy and consciousness gifted from creation* to support the divine soul plan of this planet (to learn to love) and all things within and upon it. The detailed teachings about these flames are available to all of humanity.

All energies of these various flames flood the planet from the higher realms each day. For the purposes of this discourse and dialogue, we shall focus on the Violet Flame from which I receive such love and support and work within.

This most magical Violet Flame of Transmutation and Freedom brings the frequency/vibration of change, alchemy, kindness, comfort and the release from limitations.

As you fill your emotions and thoughts with the wonders of this flame, its vibration will begin clearing and cleansing from your life the obstacles (wounds and ego defenses) and karmic consequence preventing your pathway to your self-mastery and ascension.

In effect, all the flames work together in perfect balance and harmony to assist your healing and your destined ascension. *Self-mastery and self-empowerment come from the dedicated application of these Flames.* You are the Creator creating your life, balancing the universal equation, Responsibility = Consequences. When you are responsible for everything in your life, you create consequences to your liking, creating the life you say you want.

These eternal and ever-lasting Flames of Creation will work for you as you do the work, working with them. No one can do the work for you, and no one can interfere with your freedom of choice and will. Spiritual growth and expansion are achieved by making them the priority of your life.

Resonating and receiving with this Violet Flame and its attributes opens the creative cosmic channels to balance giving and receiving in your lives, while better understanding the CODES OF CREATION that support your return to your divinity.

Breathe in, summon and receive this self-empowering energy. During your meditation or when out in nature, connect with the energy of this Violet Flame that will connect you with your higher self as well as we of the Ascended Master Realms.

By connecting with this fabulous flame you will diminish the dimensional walls that separate us. You will clearly see your divine purpose in being here. I am ever ready and present to be with you. You simply have to *open your heart and ask, and you will receive.*

Your Teacher & Friend,

St Germain

DISCOURSE #3

WAKE UP AND CLAIM YOUR DIVINITY!

Beloved Students,

Many of you are aware you are moving from the worn out old to an unknown new. At this gifted time of ascension of your planet and yourselves, you are being given a divine gift to awaken to your true selves and purpose in being here (to learn to love, as the "Loveversity" of Creation).

If you choose, it is time to let go of duality and confrontation that still holds your world captive. Together, let us now *join in Oneness and We consciousness to fully activate your divine soul plans* for both the planet and the people.

I, St. Germain, who once walked the Earth like you now, am a vital link to this personal process of moving from the mercurial Me to the wondrous We. As you awaken further, more is being revealed beyond your organized religions, governments, corporations and erroneous belief systems. Together, we are destined to be the sons and daughters of Source, ALL THERE IS.

Recently my divine soul plan has been ushering in the I AM PRESENCE from the Piscean into the Aquarian ages. During this channel's birth month, August, 2016, you once again experienced the Harmonic Convergence where several of your solar system's planets aligned to energetically assist your ascension process.

This cosmic event further allowed the integration of your I AM Presence within your third dimensional reality of emotions, thoughts and physicality. NEITHER MAN NOR ANY OTHER BEING CAN NOW SHUT THIS UNIFIED PORTAL. This created a balancing of personal and planetary karma where you eventually will no longer need to learn from karma (karma being a learning tool, not a punishment). It is your divine birthright for this event to take place now.

The Piscean Age is represented by two fish swimming in opposite directions. These represent the lower and the higher self that are in opposition to one another that are evolving through duality. In effect, the lower and the higher selves during the last 2,000-year cycle have been evolving in duality. As a result of the ascension process of the planet, you are evolving to a state where now the two (higher and lower selves) can unite into the Aquarian Age (represented by the water bearer, balancing the emotional and mental bodies to manifest Unity/We Consciousness). This balance will insure the awakening of the human soul.

Gratitude for this event can and will produce abundance, employing the cosmic equation: Gratitude = Abundance. As I have shared, I have had many incarnations on this planet always assisting humanity in ascending onward and upward. My mission is to reveal to each of you your true purpose as light bearers and way showers in world service leading to universal service.

As has been explained, this planet is a unique divine experiment in the universe reflected in your diversified races, languages, cultures, sexual preferences and gender, which are all becoming united. And you all signed on for the experiment. How do you think and feel you have done so far?

Through the teachings I and other higher realms are bringing once again into the world, you can directly know your higher self as your divine self as you continue to heal your wounds and ego defenses around those wounds—as well as negative karma from past and present lives.

In an earlier discourse and dialogue, we discussed The Violet Flame, which utilizes the Law of Transformation and the I AM Presence. This Flame is giving humanity worldwide the opportunity to become free of false prophets, false pastors, false gurus and false Christs in your religions, governments and corporations. Through the intentions and energies of Ascended Mastership, the truth will set you free.

The I AM Presence lives within each of you, and the Violet Flame energies are available all the time for the asking. If all the ways that separate you could know and accept this truth, peace and Oneness would come to this world!

If you so choose, now is the time to know and stop the usually hidden forces that keep humanity pitted against itself for profit and greed. The solution lies within yourselves, not outside. Your ascension process is one of awakening inside out (not outside in), a process of you being the Creator creating all that is and all that is not. You are not only All That Is but you are all that will ever be and is yet to be. This is who you are!

All that I speak of is forever present through your I AM Presence. No one and no thing can take this away from you. Are you ready to wake up and claim your divine self? Know you are in the process of accepting this now.

Your I AM Presence is creation being undifferentiated consciousness until it connects with a soul like you and activates your divine soul plan (your purpose to be here). As has been said many times, the purpose of all physical evolution is to learn to love. Remember, your unique part of creation is learning how to master being human and to transcend that reality.

Please know, we of the Ascended Masterships realms are ever present, and we shall never leave you until we are united. Soon you will graduate from this "Loveversity" having mastered being human in order to transcend this reality into your true state of divine beingness.

Your Teacher & Friend,

St Germain

DISCOURSE #4

CODES OF CREATION TO SUPPORT YOUR ASCENSION

Beloved Students,

As explained earlier, we Ascended Masters who once walked this Earth as humans for many millennia have sent *Codes of Creation* to support your moving into a higher frequency/consciousness of existence.

Since 2016, Star Seed energies from the twelve-star systems that seeded this planet have been coming into the Earth plane on a monthly basis. *This discourse and dialogue will review the twelve codes, plus a thirteenth that will be your planet when it ascends.*

As your planet continues to contract and expand during its final 2,000-year ascension cycle, humanity also is being given wondrous opportunities to ascend from a dense carbon based reality to light. This is your destiny, and how and when you get there is up to you through your free will. Those of you who choose not to ascend during this planet's final epoch will do so elsewhere.

As has been explained, your personal ascension process is a process of inside out (not outside in) based upon your healed relationship with self (self being a reflection of ALL THERE IS).

Looking at your outside world is not a measure of the process. Remember, you will also contract and expand. Your ascension is not always a straight forward path. It is essential that you know that what is occurring is something you chose on a higher level. What you are experiencing is not any form of punishment but the way you chose to facilitate your mastership.

Each *Code of Creation* is an energetic intention/portal representing those twelve-star systems with the final Code being you and your planet's ascension itself.

Codes of Creation

used in Treatment 6/22/19

1. I intend to heal all wounds and ego defenses created from past and present lives. I remember these are not me, but they often rule my life and world at present. I have been given many tools from higher realms to assist in my healing. Am I ready to finally do the work and apply them? My healing will allow my direct connection with the ascended master realms and become them.

used in Treatment 7/21/19

2. I intend to know and apply the meaning, value and purpose of being within this third dimension of emotions, thoughts and physicality. Each dimension has a purpose; my purpose is to learn to love through duality and to transcend into world service through unity. Lower frequencies are not allowed within the higher realms. My mission is to raise my frequency through consciousness.

used in Treatment 7/20

3. I intend to transmute my believing mind into service of my knowing heart. Stored within the DNA of my heart is all I need to know from past and present experiences. My self-mastered self is alive and well within my heart, and I am learning to think with my heart. I am in a process of learning how to access this.

used in Treatment 7/23/19

4. I intend to know that duality, separation and confrontation are an illusion and not my ascended state of being. I shall wake up and remember there is no two, only one. I choose to release the pain and suffering this illusion has caused and not need to learn through it any more.

5. I intend to remember and apply the truth that all judgment, shaming and blaming in my world is simply how I feel about myself reflecting out to others.

used in Treatment 7/24/19

6. I intend to surrender to not knowing even though my mental body thinks it knows. In the not knowing are all possibilities and probabilities living in the void of creation. My knowing heart contains all I need to know. I am learning how to access this.

combine w/ #13

7. I intend to know that my ascension is the marriage/union of my eternal self, my I AM Presence, with Creation. I shall achieve this union through the healing of the self-centered me into the healed we. *yet Love Me*

8. I intend to remember that I agreed to a human contract on this planet to understand, access and apply my divinity within every moment of the now.

9. I intend to acknowledge that every human being, animal, plant, mineral and unseen being on this planet are conscious beings made of the same cosmic elements and have a divine right to be here. They are not meant to be controlled by me. Trying to control anyone or anything is a reflection of my non-loving relationship with myself.

10. I intend to realize that my emotions are creating the life I am having. My emotions create thoughts which create actions. My emotions are stored in the atmosphere creating weather.

11. I intend to experience joy knowing it is one of the highest frequencies within the universe. Joy is an empowering aspect of love, the building block of the universe. The feeling of joy allows manifestation with grace and ease. I intend to pay attention to how much joy is presently in my life.

12. I intend to be conscious of my ascension process, moving from density to light. This process is achieved by two factors: First, I know I came from love, I am love, and I am lovable, and I intend to mirror this out into the world; Second, I intend to have gratitude for what *is* in my life rather than focus in on what is *not*. I am mastering the cosmic equation: Gratitude = Abundance.

13. I intend to commit to be willing to do the work to release myself from myself. All the tools I need have been given to me from higher realms many times. I am ready to commit to my ascension and see it as the most important aspect of my life.

Your Teacher & Friend,

St Germain

DISCOURSE #5

THE ASCENSION CHAIR, MY GIFT TO YOU

Beloved Students,

Many of you may have heard of The Ascension Chair or experienced one of the Ascension Chair ceremonies that this channel has facilitated over the years. For those not familiar with this sacred ceremony (that you can do on your own at any time), please allow this to be a discourse and dialogue to bring deeper understanding of this amazing ascension tool. The detailed instructions as to how to create this ceremony yourself are at the end of this discourse and dialogue.

The Ascension Chair is a glorious gift from my beloved heart to this "Loveversity" called Earth and to all you divine human beings on the surface of this planet. *Quite simply, this is a tool to assist the raising of frequency/vibration of any candidate for ascension.*

The energetic structure of The Ascension Chair contains the frequency of the pure white light of the Ascension Flame, which raises an individual's vibration gradually and gently. While sitting in a designated chair you will only receive what you can maintain and sustain at that moment. For the purposes of this discourse and dialogue I am focusing only on the Violet Flame, one of the Seven Sacred Flames.

If you were to receive the full force of the Ascension Flame (which you are not ready for in your evolution at this time), your dense carbon body would be transmuted into its light body, and you could achieve permanent ascension into the higher realm I reside within now (fifth dimensional consciousness). Anything less than love and light dissolves, and the candidate is instantly transformed and reconnected with the fullness of their Divine Essence, allowing all spiritual gifts and attributes restored. An individual must be spiritually ready on all levels to achieve this. This is the divine destination that you will achieve (when ready) that so many of you long for at this time. What awaits you is a permanent union of your unhealed self with your higher, healed divine self.

Again, facilitating an Ascension Chair Ceremony is a wonderful way to increase your frequency (within a loving community) as much as you can at this time within your evolutionary process. The more you experience the ceremony, the higher your frequency becomes each time.

While the Ascension Chair is a tremendous gift, it is not the only way you can achieve ascension. The higher realms have offered several "personal processing" techniques to support you. (See *Life Mastery, A Guide for Creating the Life You Want and the Courage to Live It* by Joel D. Anastasi.) **They are all based upon healing the relationship with self and mirroring that out into the world**.

In addition to the Ascension Chair Ceremonies you can set up on your own, please know there are a few fifth dimensional retreat chairs located in various locations on this planet. Facilitated by the Great White Brotherhood, I have one located at Jackson Peak, Wyoming, and there is another located within the Inner Earth Civilization of Lemuria in Telos.

If it resonates, I urge you to begin performing the Ascension Chair Ceremony yourselves. I have designed a ceremony to be easily performed by you divine beings experiencing the third dimension.

Your Teacher & Friend,

St Germain

ASCENSION CHAIR CEREMONY

The Ascension Chair is a tool to assist the raising of the vibration of a candidate for ascension. It contains the frequencies of the pure white Light of the Ascension Flame. It raises one's vibration gradually and gently.

The regular practice of this ritual with each ceremony builds a huge momentum. The energies almost double in intensity and beauty each time this sacred ceremony is performed. It affects and helps not only the people participating in the group, but also creates a web of Light touching almost the entire planet.

As you evolve your consciousness, The Ascension Flame helps your purification process in greater measure each time and assists in the raising of your vibration every time you express your intention through this sacred ritual.

Each person comes forth to sit on the chair to declare their intention vocally before their friends and before their God to express their desire and intention for ascension. The candidate also declares the willingness to do whatever it takes to make this happen. Ascension has been defined by the Sacred Flame Masters as the "union of your human self with your Eternal Spiritual Being."

As the candidate formulates an intention, a prayer, Master St Germain floods the individual's force field with the level of ascension frequency appropriate for that person in the now moment.

THE CEREMONY

We gather chairs in a circle around a designated Ascension Chair, and each person comes forth to sit on the chair and states their intention, preferably aloud with a fully open heart, their goals for this life and for their ascension. Make the most honorable prayer your heart dictates or inspires you to express at this moment. (Those who cannot think of anything in the moment may select a card from the Lemurian messages and read it aloud).

Each person holds a special crystal in their hand (provided by the facilitator) and sits on the chair for about three to five minutes.

When finished the candidate gives a sign of completion with their eyes (to the facilitator), the facilitator or designated person rings the Tibetan bells once, and the group sings three "AUMs" to assist anchoring this energy in the physical while the person remains seated. Then the person returns to their seat and the next person comes forth.

There is always a natural flow created, and each one takes their turn in no specific order. The facilitator can go last. When everyone is finished several Lemurian masters invite you to drink an elixir, which they charge with the frequency of the "Golden Liquid Light." Sparkling apple juice is poured into small cups and passed to the group.

A short invocation is made to ask that the liquid each person holds in their right hand be infused with the frequency of the Golden Liquid Light. There is a pause to allow the masters to transform the liquid at the frequency that is most appropriate for each person.

When given the signal, each person slowly drinks the liquid that has now become a sacred alchemical elixir, expressing their deep gratitude for the gift and rich blessings now bestowed upon them.

When we come together in group, in community and reinforce our intentions, it becomes more powerful in all our lives. This sacred ritual is a blessed way for like-spirited people to spend time together. This is a simple and pleasant tool to raise your consciousness. And so be it, beloved children of the heart. Be in peace and in love with yourself.

NOTE: Before the ceremony, the room is cleared and cleansed, lit with candles, low music, set with fresh flowers and the chair prepared by covering it with a fabric.

DISCOURSE #6

THE MEANING, VALUE AND PURPOSE OF ASCENSION

Beloved Students,

The meaning, value and purpose of the ascension process is to release energetic blockages (the emotional, mental and physical armoring around yourselves from past and present incarnational cycles) in order to regain the balance of energy in your bodies, a process which facilitates true and permanent healing.

The awakening of the soul is an aspect of the healing; knowing who you are and why you are here. Through the actual healing process itself, you are reconnecting and awakening with the fragments of your divine soul plan.

Trust and surrender through your resonance and discernment (your internal gyro system) that your ascension is possible and is becoming the priority in your life. Your personal ascension process is not necessarily reflected in what is going on in the outside world since this is a personal process of inside out, not outside in.

The *task is to be "in" your world not "of" it.* This is a challenge for most of you since your need for drama keeps you attached to your worldly events. *By staying attached to drama your nervous system is stimulated into a state of dense doingness, rather than focusing on the higher frequency beingness of ascension.* Ascension *beingness* will create an elevated *doingness.*

Ascension involves building a new parallel path to what you are experiencing in the old (not intersecting with the old) that extends into a higher frequency of existence beyond the old.

Regarding your current events, remember, they are an aspect of the whole (of ALL THERE IS) and not the whole. The core issue within the human contract is always about the relationship with self, mirrored outward. Remember, you are creation reflecting itself out to the world. All that is happening in your world at present is a mirror of self.

Within your human contract you have chosen to experience what *is* through what is *not*, often through duality/separation leading to confrontation. You are now experiencing exacerbations of this behavior, which appear to be the worst it has ever been. In reality, it is not. All of this needs to come up through the ascension process to heal from within. It is all in divine order no matter how things look from the outside.

We of the higher realms are all about bringing messages and tools to your frequency in order to set you free from it, to release yourself from it, which is your divine destiny. You will accept these or not through your resonance and discernment. Your truth and pathway are gained through your resonance and discernment and the emotion that you feel around these.

During this lifetime, many of you have come together again for a continuation, and, in some ways, a completion of what was started in the past. This is *a grand reunion* of like-minded and like-spirited people to support and love one another in communities of equality, harmony, and balance, supporting each other's ascension process. *This endeavor of discourses and dialogues is very much a continuation and completion of mutual soul plans.*

Your Teacher & Friend,

St Germain

DISCOURSE #7

WONDERS TO COME IN YOUR NEW GOLDEN AGE

Beloved Students,

As humanity continues its ascension process and evolves further into We consciousness, wonderful gifts will be gifted to you as you become better prepared to receive them. This is how it has always been during the creation of Golden Ages. The creation of this final Golden Age is no exception.

These ages are never created alone. They are created with the love and support from higher dimensions. Remember, humanity's separation from higher realms caused the demise of all past Golden Ages. Your ascension process now insures a permanent connection; as above, so below.

Everything in nature takes total responsibility for its place in nature and its effect. Humanity is the only creature that does not. And you have been paying a price for not being responsible, remembering the universal equation:

Responsibility = Consequence.

To bring further joy into your lives, I would like to preview some of the wonders to come and the ascension advancements you need to maintain in your consciousness in order to sustain these advancements.

USING BODY-CONSCIOUS ENERGY

This will enable humanity to power electronic/digital apparatus through brain waves by the use and mastery of the energy currents flowing through your heart and mind. Your emotions and thoughts have always created your reality; soon you will put this principle into further practice.

PHOTOGRAPHING THE UNSEEN WORLD

Cameras will become so sensitized they will photograph the human aura—your etheric, unseen, non-physical body just outside your physical body. This is the portion that maintains and sustains your physical. This will give medical physicians the ability to see the real cause and effect of many emotional, mental and physical imbalances and will permit true, permanent healing.

MAGNETISM AS A POWER SOURCE

Mastering magnetism will become possible, which will allow the suspension of objects without visible support. This is the constructive wisdom of the Ascended Masters revealed. We have mastered the manipulation of energy. There is enough unseen free energy in your world to power the entire planet. This will be a game changer for your governments, corporations and economy.

EXPANDED FORMS OF TRANSPORTATION

New forms of air/water/land navigation and transportation/teleportation will be made possible by utilizing inner and outer Earth electro-magnetic energies. Thus, objects will rise in complete resistance to gravity, and you will be free to explore the cosmos without further consuming the Earth's resources.

CONTROLLING WEATHER

Through your raised consciousness you will know your emotions and thoughts create weather. Once you become awake to the true power of your emotions and minds, you will create perfect weather. Think of the time and resources that presently are lost due to weather.

The above wonders will be dwarfed by still greater wonders to come from higher realms as you ascend into your final Golden Age.

In order to prevent humanity from repeating the past and destroying itself by the misuse of advanced technologies, I, Saint Germain, make the following suggestions to shift and change your lives to ensure your divine destiny:

1. Take full responsibility for everything you are creating in your life and the world.

2. Give up duality, separation and confrontation.

3. Give up herd consciousness.

4. Nurture all life.

5. Give up judgment, shaming and blaming.

6. Exercise acceptance, compassion and forgiveness everywhere, all the time.

7. Remember, you have free choice and will.

8. See yourself in others.

9. Know who you are and why you are here.

10. Feel your feelings and heal your emotional body.

11. Heal your mental body by reducing negative thoughts.

12. Love yourself enough to love others.

Your Teacher & Friend,

St Germain

CONCLUSION FOR THE SEVEN DISCOURSES

Beloved Students,

The more of humanity who can accept the presence of higher realms such as I, Saint Germain, the wider new doors of truth and freedom are opened and old worn out doors of separation are closed forever.

All of you who have listened to or read these discourses and dialogues please thank yourself for showing up. Know within your hearts, you now have the tools to create a new paradigm/reality through your resonance and discernment of equality, harmony and balance in your personal and world lives and to transcend those lives.

Remember that humanity never ceases creating through being the Creator. It is now time to create the life and world your truly say you want. I have given you some mighty tools to be and do during this exchange. Are you ready to accept and apply them?

Please accept with compassion and forgive how you have chosen to learn what you need to learn the way you need to learn it. Your permanent healing is assured through the choices you now make and the ascension process you chose.

We of the Ascended Master realms are complete, pure, perfect, all-powerful Divine Beings who never make mistakes. We have mastered energy and manifestation. We were human just like you and made our ascension the priority of our souls, and so can you.

We are the Wondrous Way Showers revealing all the possibilities and probabilities of what lies before you.

I shall never leave you until we permanently join hands and hearts in the higher realms.

I AM a Child of the Light.

I love the Light.

I serve the Light.

I live in the Light.

I AM protected, illuminated, supplied and sustained by the light.

I bless the light.

Your Teacher & Friend,

St Germain

TEACHINGS TO FREE HUMANITY FROM TYRANTS

* Negative childhood experiences inevitably shape the adult behavior of tyrants.

* Fame allows a tyrannical leader to be both charming and frightening at the same time. He uses it as a means of influence and control.

* Tyrants feel justified in crushing anyone and anything in their path which would hinder their great "destiny."

* Many controlling leaders stand alone, without the need for friends they cannot trust. The most important thing in their lives is their "destiny" which must be fulfilled at all cost.

* No Superman or Master Race can control what they did not create. All advanced civilizations on this planet were achieved with the support of the higher realms.

* Tyrants have the ability to make complex problems appear simple, often reducing them to a misleading answer of true or false. If lies are told long enough, you may believe them—even the lie that one aspect of humanity is responsible for all the evils of the world. This is how hatred can become acceptable.

* Tyrants are blind to how their behavior affects others because of their need to control.

* The tyrant exploits political, cultural, religious and racial divisions to his advantage and his own personal success.

* Tyrants seek to create unrest, struggle and hate in their nation and often in other nations. They poison relations between peoples of countries by envy, hatred, struggle and warfare. The watchwords are force and hypocrisy.

* The tyrant paints the deeds of foreign governments with lies and confrontations and creates so much ill-feelings towards them that the people would rather bear slavery which offers order and peace than have freedom.

* The tyrant blames others for the ills of life, turning counter-revolution into a spiritual crusade, even converting the deeply held religious beliefs of the people to his cause.

* The tyrant's voice echoes with magical, mystical powers that can seduce people into a reduced state of moral responsibility and simultaneously excite them to rise up and support untruths having no factual foundation—hoping that few people will expose or denounce him.

* If the tyrant tells lies often enough, one day the people will accept him and his lies as their benefactor and savior.

* The tyrant depends on the ignorance and arrogance of the public.

* There is no true love and peace in the being of the tyrant.

* The tyrant thinks he has a master-plan that cannot fail, but his ruthlessness prevents any workable plan.

* Sexual, physical and emotional confusion and distortion creates a rage within the tyrant that is reflected in all his relationships. This behavior can affect governmental actions.

* The cosmic chronicle, the eternal tapestry of world destiny, is always in perfect divine order with the past, present and future, inseparably woven into the now.

* At present, millions of humans are waking up through the evolution of human consciousness. This is the role of the tyrant. An individual spiritual identity is being born which is integrating into a collective consciousness with a new sense of love, peace, equality, harmony and balance that transcends myopic forms of nationalism.

* The tyrant teaches humanity the futility of misplaced patriotism and unquestioning loyalty to the leaders of the nation.

* The tyrant attempts to disempower and excommunicate anyone or anything within their path.

* Do not underestimate the "occult dark magic" training and practices of many tyrants. They depend on you not believing that they exist. Practicing ritual magic can create unconscious tools of higher powers that can unleash horrors on humanity. The Western mind finds it challenging to accept the existence of any kind of magic as a reality. This is because the basic concept behind all magical practice is a belief in a connection between the universe and humanity (between the macrocosm and microcosm). The Western mind, based in materialism, finds such thinking unscientific. The motivating power in all magical endeavors is the trained will of the magician moving into pure energy; then the properly trained human will is capable of many things.

* Beware of the hypnotic magnetism of the tyrant who plays on your wounds and ego defenses.

* The tyrant often fuses religion and politics together to support their image of the world. They fear the division of church (often a corrupted view of spirituality) and state.

* Often the tyrant goes through a distorted transmutation where he proclaims himself the true and only leader. He joins hands with his wounds and ego defenses in a mission to vanquish the free spirit of humanity—often inflicting the greatest crimes against his own people.

* The mission of the tyrant is to build a regime where no one will disagree or turn against him. This is accomplished through fear and threats. This illusion will ultimately destroy the tyrant who will blame others for his downfall. You cannot control what you did not create.

* Because of the childhood wounds and the defenses surrounding those wounds, the tyrant cannot bear good will toward anyone. He can only rob them of any joy (especially those most honored and respected around him) in ways that make him feel good.

* Most tyrants achieve some form of transcendent consciousness through the use of drugs. Because of the tyrant's imbalanced nature, the drugs often have a negative effect. Great lengths are used to hide this.

* The tyrant does everything he can to gain a large section of the academic and professional world to support his distorted views of reality. If they do not cooperate, he will make it up.

* The tyrant builds an inner circle that he hopes he can trust. Because of internal disagreements, leaks occur, exposing the tyrant and creating his fury.

* High above the world and beyond the reach of the masses, the tyrant is enthroned in gold, living in his illusion of domination and control fueled by hate and on the verge of insanity, ultimately seeking revenge on everyone. Since you cannot control what you did not create, all these feelings will one day destroy the tyrant.

* The tyrant often believes intellectuals are in the way of his mission. He believes he is the action figure of a necessary revolution in policy and morals and that he is the instrument of humanity's re-orientation, a new age reflecting his interpretation of nation and world—an interpretation based upon will, not intelligence.

*Tyrants often believe they are the reincarnation of a past ruler here to complete a mission.

* Tyrants often have some physical symbol of their power—be it wealth, a whip, etc. These symbols reflect an unhealed ego and its fruit: arrogance, resentment, bullishness, contempt for anyone or anything standing in their way (sociopath), insecurity, self-deceit and hate.

* Even when praising others, the tyrant is so self-centered he can only praise himself.

* The first condition for success for most tyrants is a complete knowledge of the weaknesses and vices of his opponents.

* The tyrant believes he can only achieve his goals by the systematic corruption of the influential and governing classes. He employs

power-politics with a brutal force and does not care if he uses every lie possible to gain his ends.

* The tyrant's ability to "bewitch" an audience with his speaking skills, lashing out at others, hits the hearts of those who resonate with his message. It's all about inflicting unrestrained emotions of hatred (not content or truth) with no restraint. He is giving everyone permission to feel and express the same hatred. Promising to fulfill their needs later does not matter. What matters is the moment. Pay attention to me, like me, love me. The power of the spoken word is his weapon, power of oratory (performance) holding the audience spellbound; actual substance or content is meaningless.

* The tyrant appeals to the most secret desires, the least acceptable instincts, the suffering and the personal revolts of the nation. "I am one of you, hear my roar." Meanwhile, the tyrant may be living in a golden tower, but that no longer matters. The audience is seduced and ready for the climax.

* The tyrant speaks as spirit moves him, with no need of a script. He is transformed as the "messiah" of the many. He feels/smells the atmosphere of the room and feeds those feelings to his audience. His words are a gun shot into the heart of the wounds of others telling the masses what they want to hear the way they would say it.

* Shooting from the hip and speaking and acting from an instinctive nature, the tyrant is most often unable to control or direct his vison.

* The tyrant often appears on the stage of the evolution of humanity to teach what "is" through what is "not", attempting to blind humanity to their individual and collective divine soul plan and destination.

* The tyrant often realizes to what extent the contemporary world is asleep to the real meaning of historical process. History is something the living have helped to create in former lives on earth.

* Every thousand years or so all that needs to be cleared and cleansed is set loose from its prison.

* A tyrant's life can become the salvation of an entire nation. The tyrant can become a proxy acting through karma.

* Tyrants often adopt an aggressive territorial view justifying international bullying on a global scale, a blueprint for world domination.

* Every person in some way is an actor on the stage of world politics. The world would be incomplete without each of you.

* Looking at the push and pull of the ascension process of this planet and humanity, it is revealing to see the manner in which hierarchies of evil (imbalance) or good (balance) can oppose or support the ascension of human consciousness within each epoch. Now with the planet in its final 2000-year ascension cycle, the positive and negative forces are accelerating.

* Often the tyrant feels he has been chosen to move humanity from its intellectual inertness by his own hands. He promises he will bring about the redemption and improvement of every aspect of life but has no idea how or plan to fulfill this promise.

* The idea of a personal "savior or messiah" appearing has dominated human thinking for ages. Humanity is now learning that any messianic revelations will be a process of inside out, not outside in.

* Most tyrants see no guilt in their actions and feel the "gods of the cosmic court" will acquit them of any crime. This is their insanity.

This is the aspect of humanity that is healing within the ascension process.

* The occult and satanic nature of many tyrants is hidden from humanity who can only accept the outward aspects of the behavior of these individuals.

* Within any higher realm initiate training, when the human third eye has been opened, you can access a full vision of the Akashic Record (containing all wisdom) and see the whole evolution of human, world and universal events.

* What you are experiencing at present can be called a "personality cult" in which personal ambition is being inflamed to extremes. The greater the personal power of the tyrant the more he wishes to exploit it. It is the egotistical abuse of power that will bring down the tyrant.

* Through feeling and thinking humanity can compare experiences, improvise and improve things. As a result of emotions and thoughts, the faculty of moral choices arises which can check and balance the otherwise insatiable powers of instinct, impulse and desire. Only through the application of such feeling and thinking powers and a capacity to connect to the inner voice of conscience can you end the egotistical satisfaction of perverse appetites which can destroy a nation.

* The tyrant intends to gain mastery over nature so the despiritualized intellect can reign supreme. As untruth becomes the call of the day, he intends to create an ever-widening gap between truth and reality and spirit and matter.

* The tyrant does not know nor care that the Earth is a conscious living organism, a kind of giant reflection in all aspects of the human

being itself—the emotional, mental and physical components of humanity finding its exact counterpart in the Earth-Being.

* The consciousness of early humanity could have remained an infallible mirror image of the "perfected" world, but this aim was diverted by a hierarchy of opposing powers (Lucifer and Ahriman) who sought to evoke a resistance to this truth. Humanity felt, by severing the direct connection to the macrocosm, he could do it a better way. This allowed these denser energies to come in. The human "I" or "ego" fell into dependence upon denser elements in the soul. Thus, the free choice was made to learn this way.

* Lucifer and Ahriman forces/energies are the two primary "teaching tools" of humanity's ascension/evolution process. Lucifer leads man into a spiritual independence of the higher realms, setting himself up as a (false) god. Ahriman's mission is to create a mainly material world which is isolated from the higher realms, allowing humanity to lose all consciousness of his spiritual origins, connection and destiny. The tyrant often applies these either consciously or unconsciously.

* The Nuremberg Trials at the end of WWII, which cost some twenty-five million lives, exposed many of the horrors of that war, but most refused to acknowledge the occult training and evil intent of the Nazi Occult Bureau. The world was not ready for a serious public investigation into occult rites, rituals and initiations that took place. Is the world ready now to know such forces exist within humanity and are at play again in your world at present?

* The cosmic conflict between the hierarchies of Light and Dark continue to play out in the ascension and destiny of humanity. Within the free will and choice of humanity, this is how you have chosen to learn what you need to learn, the way you need to permanently learn

it. You cannot know the existence of light without the darkness, or so it seems.

* This channel's first spiritual teacher was the Austrian philosopher Rudolf Steiner, who was the proxy of the Cosmic Christ Consciousness and the way shower of the eternal significance of the "Spiritual Self," which seeks to re-birth in your souls at this final ascension age of your planet. Through higher realm connections, Steiner was able to reveal and warn humanity of many of the tyrannical behaviors of the past.

* Steiner was given the gift and vision of direct connection with the higher realms that inspire the constantly changing challenges of humanity through evolving ages. Steiner saw the dual nature of the human soul. He saw how one aspect of his personality was dominated by intellect and confined him to sense-only knowledge. The other aspect of his soul connected directly with the super-sense world of spirit above and within the kingdoms of the planet. Steiner (who died in 1925) revealed the multi-dimensional aspects of humanity that you are all becoming.

* Steiner saw how the division of the soul was reflected universally in the tragic duality between science and religions (creating the chaos and conflict at present). This is why I made sure there was a division of church and state within the creation of The United States of America. The tyrant loves to play these two entities against one other for his benefit.

* It has been an essential aspect of the divine soul plan of humanity that you are completely cut off from the spiritual (macrocosm) and dwell completely within the isolation of the 3D (microcosm) world. Only through isolation from the divine could humanity develop the necessary self-mastery consciousness and freedom which are the

prerequisites for the appearance of love, peace, equality, harmony and balance on Earth. All is in divine perfect order no matter how things appear in your outside world. You are in the process of reaching your divine destination. Where are you within it now?

* The most prominent feature of the tyrant is an endless capacity to counterfeit (lie) and dissemble (divide and conquer) to make something look like what it is not and to create multiple justifications to cover up self-serving motives. Protecting your free press can expose all this. Join in a collective-consciousness to not resist the tyrant (which is what he wants and will fuel him) but to create a positive, parallel path that exceeds any intention of the tyrant for the good of all.

GLOSSARY

ASCENDED MASTER TEACHINGS, TERMS & TOOLS TO AWAKEN YOU TO YOUR DIVINITY AND HELP YOU ACHIEVE MASTERY

This is a simplified, concise reference to be used with the Seven Ascension Discourses.

This endeavor honors all that has preceded it and contains definitions and terminology that the average person can quickly access and understand during these times of change and chaos.

Each of these phrases contains an energetic entrainment to raise your consciousness and vibrations.

A CONSTRUCTIVE PERSONAL PROCESS allowing a deep examination and healing of the wounded self will allow the Ascended Master to come forth, pouring out courage, strength and love. (See Life Mastery, A Guide for Creating the Life You Want and the Courage to Live It.)

A CUSTODIAN OF LIFE is who all humans are; taking responsibility for being a creator is essential; after self-mastery, taking self out into world service through your talents and gifts; being the **Book of Life**.

A DOUBT need only be felt a couple of times until it becomes distrust; distrust spins in the emotional body and becomes suspicion; suspicion is self-destruction.

A FATHER'S HOUSE: Seeking to realize the ecstatic joy and perfection within the God self is required to become an Ascended Master student, turning your back on the human senses and holding your attention to the universal Source of ALL THERE IS.

A HUGE GIFT OF THE ASCENDED STATE is the complete absence of any judgment or shaming of human lack and limitations.

A REAL MASTER will never identify themselves as a master, nor accept payment of any kind; their free gift is their service of love to the world; they will, however, assist in creating themselves in others.

A STRONG STUDENT stands against the world of fear, doubt and ignorance and is ready to witness the activities of God manifested by the Ascended Masters.

A TINY BIT OF LOVE AND GRATITUDE TO YOUR I AM PRESENCE will transmute any and every unhappiness in your life, releasing the perfection of life.

ACCEPTING THE TEACHING AND LOVE of the Ascended Masters and other higher realms is essential at this time, trusting their words (beyond the human mind), their promises and truth.

ACCUMULATED WEALTH cannot be achieved without the assistance and radiation of some Ascended Master.

ACKNOWLEDGMENT OF LIFE AND LIGHT maintains and sustains life-giving energy; denial of it shuts off the energetic flow.

AFFIRMATION brings you to the point where you have a deep realization of the truth.

AFTER ASCENDED MASTER CONTACT there is only one over-whelming desire in life, and that is to be what they are.

ALL CONSTRUCTIVE DESIRE is the God-self within reflecting perfection into use.

ALL CREATION COMES FROM COSMIC LIGHT, a universal substance (spirit); this is the pure life substance of God, an infinite energy you may call upon for whatever you wish to manifest; this pure cosmic light is the limitless powerhouse of the universe containing all perfection creating all there is.

ALL CREATION is by self-conscious effort taking responsibility for self and not resting till perfection is reached.

ALL ENERGY has the inherent quality of perfection within it and intends to serve the creator, you.

ALL FORMS contain life.

ALL HUMAN REALTIONSHIPS are a creation within the physical world of feelings, thoughts, words and action; in the ascended state all is united in we consciousness, a unified field of oneness.

ALL IMPULSES of consciousness return back to the point that sent them; nothing escapes this truth.

ALL KNOWING MIND, ALL SEEING EYE OF GOD is the Ascended Master.

ALL KNOWLEDGE can be obtained when the motive is pure and unselfish.

ALL MANKIND IS DESTINED to know all that is contained within this glossary and elsewhere; each of you has the master God self and I AM Presence within you right now.

ALL MUST ACCOMPLISH mastery from the physical side of life; all ascensions take place consciously through the healing of self.

ALL PERFECT cannot create imperfection; free will determines what a person creates with given life energy.

ALL POWER becomes the willing servant of self-mastery; all universal forces are awaiting our command when it is for the good of all.

ALL POWERFUL MANIFESTERS are the Ascended Masters, since all elements are their willing and obedient servants.

ALWAYS IN ACTION is the I AM Presence; humanity is learning to accept the use of this like the Ascended Masters; this is the Christ Consciousness and the only consciousness in creation that can say "I AM."

AMAZON means "boat destroyer," an ancient memory of the great Earth flood.

AMERICA BELONGS TO GOD; it is the anchor that fastens the God control of land.

AMERICA IS BLESSED beyond any other nation on the planet, and due to her great blessings, she is destined to share a great light in the world; the Ascended Master priority work in America is important in healing the entire Earth.

AMERICA IS THE REMAINING HOPE OF HUMANITY. America is the way shower for the rest of the world; the destiny of America reflects the oneness destiny of the world; America cannot be saved by any human hand; it can only be saved by the hand of God's love and power, the I AM Presence.

AMERICA STAND UP, the way shower of the world, demands the end of constant misrepresentation; we the people, by and for the people must rule, and bring this out into the world; demand your America be filled with the Ascended Master sacred fire of eternal freedom.

AN INNATE IDEA AND IDEAL is the ascended human body transmuted into the eternal ascended state, immortal, all wise, forever youthful and beautiful.

ANGEL MASTER is another beloved name for Ascended Masters.

ANOTHER WAY TO EXPLAIN ACTUAL ASCENSION is by way of mechanically accelerating the atomic frequency of the physical body, raising the pure electronic body.

ANY DECREE OF LIFE that accepts less than limitless perfection is not the plan of God and will continue to be a destructive force in the world; all ascension students will feel great joy when they embrace this truth.

ANYTHING AND EVERYTHING THAT HAPPENS is a reflection of the unbalanced or repressed energy of the people; people have not yet understood how they are creating; this teaching is explaining what needs to be learned.

APPETITE is but habit established by the continued gratification of the feeling nature; it is energy focused and qualified by suggestions from the personal activity of life.

AS HUMANITY WAKES UP they will lose their need to kill one another and any other life forms as well; the planet is destined to return to a garden of paradise, obedient to Divine Wisdom.

ASCENDED MASTER HUMAN MATERIAL is a student willing to be and do what is necessary to heal the unhealed personal self and to fully cooperate with an Ascended Master, doing work beyond the human experience.

ASCENDED MASTERS ARE READY to give us protection, but the strength of the God power you must recognize within yourself in order for the masters to release it; the masters will withdraw from those who make another choice.

ASCENDING THE PHYSICAL BODY is best achieved by allowing the human reproductive seed to primarily be used to create another human. Other times, this seed-energy can be used by connecting with your I AM Presence through the crown chakra; through uplifting emotions and thoughts an individual can achieve creative work through their unique talents and gifts and bring these out into the world in service.

ASCENSION INTENTION: "Beloved I AM Presence, which I surely am, take charge in full mastery this body. Let me willfully and consciously come and go from my body; never again allow it to bind me or limit my freedom."

ASSISTANCE FROM ASCENDED MASTERS often comes from the expression of human talents and gifts, doing creative work and bringing that out into the world; this is the way Ascended Masters work impersonally.

ATTITUDE TO WORK WITH AN ASCENDED MASTER is a student willing to purify, discipline and perfect themselves in order to become an expression of divine love, wisdom and power to assist in their work.

ATTRACTING FORCE BETWEEN ATOMS is love, the directive force that wills form into existence.

ATTRIBUTES OF GOD SELF are the activity of seeing and the power to create, which is within you constantly.

BECOME FRIENDS WITH YOUR MIGHTY MASTER WITHIN as you would a lover who possesses unlimited, unconditional love and power; it is your destiny to become this master.

BECOME THE LOVE that does not intend to possess; then love is truly divine.

BECOMING AN ASCENDED MASTER IS NOT SO DIFFICULT if you allow yourself, without the constant resistance, to be in the flow of your divinity, to see yourself worthy and good enough to embrace your divine essence; this is your natural birthright.

BECOMING AN ETERNAL FOUNTAIN OF DIVINE LOVE is the mission of humanity.

BEING A CHANNEL OF HIGHER REALMS is a soul plan choice of the person and the realm; some channels have more gifts and understanding than others; it is essential to know and see only God being expressed; higher realms bless all sincere actions.

BEING INFALLIBLE is the true nature of the Ascended Master; having transmuted from the frequency where mistakes can occur, by raising their vibration, limitless creation is available through the love of God.

BELOVED ASCENDED MASTER SAINT GERMAIN is the emissary from the Great White Brotherhood bringing divine protection to this planet, especially into America, leading the world into a new paradigm of unity consciousness.

BLAZING OUTPOURINGS OF LIGHT is what Ascended Masters are, freed from all human limitations where no human discord may enter.

BREATH OF GOD is the never-ending vibration/frequency of creation; this is the strongest activity of love

BY ACCEPTING AND APPLYING the I AM Presence, humanity can at any time manifest the highest good into their lives.

CATACLYSMS IN NATURE are the way the planet returns to humanity its misuse of universal substance, returning this misuse to its Source through storms and "acts of god."

CAUSE AND EFFECT is a balancing process governing all forces in creation.

CHANCE AND ACCIDENT do not exist; every experience has a cause, and everything is the cause of a future effect.

CHANGING BODIES is a natural function of Ascended Masters, since cellular structure is always under their conscious control; every atom is obedient to their command.

COMING OF CHRIST was an initiation to the world and a cosmic command to use the divine power of love in all activities called the Cosmic Divine Blueprint, awakening Christ within all.

COMPLETE OBEDIENCE of the personal self to the I AM Presence needs to be constantly maintained and sustained; this behavior illuminates and purifies the emotional, mental and physical bodies.

CONQUERING DEATH by complete dominion over the atomic substance of the physical body has been the achievement of the Ascended Masters; all things obey their command; universal laws are their servants.

CONSCIOUS DIVINE DESIRE is God in action within you; if desire was not in God's laws, manifestation would not have ever taken place; desire activity is the ever-expanding motion of life itself; know the difference between desire and human appetite.

CONSCIOUS DOMINION OF THE GOD MIND is required to be a student of an Ascended Master; many are called but few are chosen.

CONSCIOUS INTELLIGENCE is the only presence and power that can move or do anything constructive, which acknowledges its own being and manifestation by stating "I AM," followed by whatever quality that being desires to manifest into physical existence.

CONSCIOUS MASTERY is complete conscious control of your emotions, thoughts and physical body and the ability to use free will all the time.

CONSCIOUS SELF-CORRECTION occurs when a person awakens, attaining consciousness, and then nothing can prevent right action.

CONSCIOUS THOUGHT is determined by the number of electrons which combine with one another in a specific atom; the frequency at which electrons spin is determined by feelings.

CONSTANTLY DIRECTED DIVINE LOVE becomes—in action—love, wisdom and power; this is the importance of divine conscious direction; manifestation becomes instant as soon as any misdirected consciousness ceases to exist.

CONSTRUCTIVE DESIRE is the conscious direction of limitless God energy through wisdom (applied knowledge).

CONTINENT OF MERU was the name of ancient South America and the name of a great cosmic master.

CONTINENT OF MU, Lemuria, will rise and once more bring advanced knowledge into the world.

CONTINUING LIFETIMES OF LIMITATION is what humanity is learning to prevent; when love and perfection are fully expressed with the understanding that the purpose of life is to love, there will be no further need for repeated Earth lives, as you have known them.

CORRECTION of the human self is the only path to mastery.

COSMIC ASCENSION CYCLE now is allowing Ascended Masters to give more than ordinary support; great outpourings of light are coming into Earth, purifying and balancing human abuse, to cleanse the planet and to protect future life upon and within the planet.

CURIOSITY on the part of the ascension student need be totally eliminated before certain understanding, power and experiences are allowed to be given on the path to mastery; curiosity is of the ego mind; trust and surrender are required.

DEMAND YOUR DISCONNECTION from anything that is a disturbance in the world around you; your ascension process is one of inside out, not outside in; demand your freedom from anything not of God.

DEMISE OF GOLDEN AGES occurs when civilizations move into a state of lethargy and release manifesting by their God power within and through their connection to higher realms.

DENYING GOD, the source of all life, can only exist as long as the allotted energy received can sustain life; denying God shuts off life-giving energy.

DESIRE is the expanding activity of God through which manifestation is constantly sustained and perfecting, enlarging itself.

DESTRUCTIVE FEELING is the greatest misdeed in the universe, creating humanity's lack and limitation.

DESTRUCTIVE WORDS create non-construction.

DIRECTLY FROM UNIVERSAL SUBSTANCE Ascended Masters create; they exist only within the Christ light; since they were once human, their promise is to way-show us into ascension, no matter what.

DISCORDANT ACTIVITIES arrive in the world through negative feelings and thoughts.

DISSOLVING KARMA is a powerful aspect of the **Violet Flame**; it creates wondrous beauty due to its power and love frequencies; it can be used in prayer, meditation and breathing techniques, taking this flame into every atom and cell within your body.

DISTINGUISHING TRUTH FROM NON-TRUTH is the key component which allows humanity to succeed or fail most often in life; listen to your internal gyro system, your resonance (how you feel about it) and your discernment, (how you think about it); these will allow you to determine the truth.

DIVINE GODS AND GODDESSES must forever be above all temptation to misuse knowledge and power.

DIVINE PRESENCE appoints keepers of all treasures on every plane of life, whether light, wisdom, substance or physical riches.

DIVINE PRESENCE is the mighty master within, the God-self of every human; its power is released in the world through the individual.

DURING THE PLANET'S EXPANSION OF LIGHT, it is essential for individuals to maintain and sustain constant control over their feelings, thoughts and spoken words; focus on being constructive, not destructive; it is imperative that take place at this crucial time.

EACH INDIVIDUAL COMES TO KNOW when they attain their consciousness/awakening by the use of their own effort/energy through feeling it; An Ascended Master cannot and will not interfere with this process, allowing the freedom of choice and will of the individual.

EACH INDIVIDUAL, through their feelings and thoughts, has the power to rise to the highest expression of self or fall to lowest; each person alone determines their divine journey of experience.

EACH PERSON IS A UNIQUE INDIVIDUAL; yet, these individuals use one universal mind, substance, wisdom and power; this is how there is but one mind, one God, one substance and one power being acted upon by the individual.

EACH PERSON is a vital link in the necklace of the chain of perfection; the I AM Presence always works in perfection.

EGYPT rose to great advancement through the right use of knowledge and power, applying humility and obedience to the God-self.

ENTERING THE CONSCIOUS PATH OF SELF MASTERY requires fully understanding the obligation to accomplish the commitment of ascension, remembering that divine love contains complete wisdom and the I AM Presence; when the student generates enough divine love and sends it out, the student's commitment is fulfilled.

ETERNAL LAW OF LIFE is: what you feel and think you bring into creation.

ETERNAL LIGHT is Creation's way of maintaining and sustaining order, peace and perfection, creating your Christ-Self.

ETERNAL ORDER OF TRUTH is "The light of God never fails"; under this law, all destructive forces will be destroyed forever.

ETERNAL TRUTH states that discord creates disintegration, which creates death.

ETERNAL YOUTH is the flame of God housed in the body of humanity; youth and beauty (aspects of love constantly coming forth in creation) can only be kept permanently by those who shut out duality.

EVERY 25,000 YEARS the higher realms that created you release a great outpouring of cosmic love, wisdom, and energy; this is taking place now.

EVERY HUMAN BEING has within them all that the Ascended Masters express, if you choose to be and do so through your free will; you are the self-determining creator creating; if you give all of your life and energy to this determination, you will succeed. What do you choose?

EVERY INDIVIDUAL IS GIFTED with the power of choice to feel, think and create experience; if constructive use of energy is used, joy and peace are created; if destructive use of energy is used, destruction returns to the individual and death can occur.

FEAR, DOUBT AND IGNORANCE are feelings whose vibrations destroy form and substance; this vibration opposes love, harmony and order; these feelings are the monsters of mankind.

FEAR in its multiple forms of expression is the prevailing feeling within humanity at present; this is the doorway through which lightless forces enter and take control of the human psyche, allowing their dark work. Fear is an absence of love; humanity is learning to love self in order to eliminate fear; learning to love is the divine mission of Earth.

FEELING ACTIVITY OF LIFE is the most unguarded aspect of human consciousness; thoughts can never become reality until they are felt through feelings.

FEELING is the actual God energy released, which manifests the truth affirmed.

FINANCIAL FREEDOM can be achieved by holding with determined determination your I AM Presence; draw it forth and use it like a limitless bank account.

FIRST STEP IN CREATION is to determine a definite, constructive plan worthy of the effort.

FOCUS your constant attention and intention upon the all-controlling God self within you; when you forget, focus there again.

FOCUSING ON PERFECTION creates perfection; your attention and intention create your reality.

FOCUSING ON THE INDWELLING POWER allows faster manifestations and ascension to follow; acceptance of the I AM Presence is a command from the Ascended Masters; hold this power until the wounded human self knows permanently that all power comes from higher realms; all life energy is gifted from the I AM Presence within.

FOR OVER 70,000 YEARS serving humanity, Saint Germain has been upholding the Flame of Freedom for this planet; for the next 2,000-year Earth cycle, he has assumed the guardianship of the Aquarian Age, moving into a world of equality, harmony and balance.

FORM FROM THE INVISIBLE TO THE VISIBLE is achieved by means of an electron, a perfect balance of light, a force field that is eternally perfect; the force field is subject to expansion and contraction; this brings substance into form from the invisible to visible.

FORM comes into existence when someone has a consciously held picture of that form; every thought contains a picture of the idea within it.

FREE WILL is a birthright.

FREE WILL is necessary for a person to be the creator creating.

GARDEN OF EDEN means divine wisdom manifesting perfection.

GLORIOUS BEINGS who love, support and guard humanity are called Ascended Masters over all that is human.

GOD ALONE IS GREAT and unto the Source of all greatness does all glory belong.

GOD ENERGY maintains and sustains all perfection, mastery and dominion over all Earthly things.

GOD IN ACTION is the activity of your emotions and thoughts expressing life in you and the world.

GOD POWER releases the energy necessary to create and express what you desire; it is the only power that ever did, does now, or ever will raise the personal self and the world.

GOD SELF association allows you to create the life you say you want.

GOD WITHIN gives the God-Self all control of outer activities.

GOD'S INTENT is abundance of all good and loving and perfect things for everyone.

GOLD is purifying, balancing the atomic structure of the world and a vitalizing high vibratory rate energy force; it is a transformer to pass the sun's power into the physical elements of the world and the life within and upon it.

GRADUATES of ascended masters graduate out of their humanity into an expanded expression of their divinity.

GREAT BATTERIES OF POWER AND ENERGY are the Ascended Masters, and whatever touches their radiance becomes highly charged; they never use any of their power to force.

GREAT COSMIC BLUEPRINT will allow humanity to remember what they once were and can choose to create again.

GREAT GOD SELF is the only real owner and controller of all wealth.

GREAT INNER GOD ACTIVITY allows you to see how perfectly and readily the outer senses merge into the inner, and the two become one.

GREAT SELFLESS ONES of the Ascended Masters have prevented humanity from destroying itself many times in the past and present.

GRIEF FOR THE DEAD or the death of a loved one is selfishness and impedes the spiritual journey that the dead one should be enjoying, resting and growing.

GUARDIANS OF HUMANITY are way-showing Ascended Masters working through the eons from invisible realms as well as the visible to awaken humanity to its divine destiny.

HAND MANEUVER of the Ascended Master is to touch the forehead with the thumb of the right hand with the fingers extending over the top of the head; this allows the appropriate level of the light radiation of the master's energy to be received.

HARMONY is love, and without it form cannot come into existence.

HEIGHT OF FOLLY is for one part of God's creation to war against another part; the desire to bless others rather than kill them is entering the hearts of humanity; selfishness that holds humanity in bondage will be replaced by forgiveness.

HIDDEN SINISTER FORCES attempting to control what they did not create, creating chaos and destruction will be completely destroyed regardless of outward appearances now; when you are ready for this to take place, humanity will return to their God presence, and peace will reign on Earth, and humanity will send out good will to all.

HIGHER REALMS ARE NOT ALLOWED to enter your world unless you call upon them; ask and yea shall receive; **Violet Flame** beings can reduce more pain and suffering by simply asking for their support on a regular basis.

HIGHER REALMS CANNOT PROTECT THAT WHICH IS NOT PURE; self-mastery and purification of self are essential within the ascension process; time to stop giving energy to destructive forces.

HIGHER REALMS OF LIFE are created of substance which is God-empowered charges of love so strong there can never be imbalance, duality or separation.

HOLY SPIRIT is the feeling component of life, Divine Love, unconditional love.

HOUR IS AT HAND when humanity must give recognition to the activity of the great Ascended Masters who constantly are loving and supporting this planet and all life upon and within it; only through the permanent connection to higher realms can humanity complete it ascension process.

HUMAN DESTRUCTIVE FEELINGS and negative thoughts have infiltrated the seen and unseen worlds with intense fear, doubt and ignorance; it is time to send other feelings and thoughts out into the world and create another reality.

HUMAN EMBODIMENT upon this planet is a gift and opportunity given to humanity to balance mistakes from past lives, learn the lessons and make another choice next time.

HUMAN LIMITATION is brought about by the failure to remember being created in the image and likeness of God.

HUMAN SENSE APPETITES often are disqualified energy that gathers through habits and patterns, which enslave until one chooses to learn love of self and others.

HUMANITY BECOMES that which his attention and intention focuses upon; if you focus on the I AM Presence, you will become the full out-picturing of that sheer perfection.

HUMANITY HAS FORGOTTEN to be grateful for all the blessings being given with life on this planet; this has prevented peace on Earth due to human selfishness.

HUMANITY IGNORES WHY THE RACE CONTINUES TO GROW OLD AND DIE; the human body cells are programmed to be eternal; only through the understanding of the flow of energy (the I AM Presence) can humanity master the cause and effect of physical death. To master death is one of the last great hurdles for humanity; the wisdom to do so is at hand; is humanity ready to accept and apply this wisdom?

HUMANITY IS LEARNING there is more in the universe than itself; this new knowledge is creating a new paradigm of equality, harmony and balance; it is becoming the new normal; new wisdom will be revealed that eliminates old untruths and will expand humanity into all there is.

HUMANITY'S HEART WANTS GOD even if their human desires seem to want something else.

HUMANITY'S LIMITATION is the result of the misuse of the God gift of free will.

IDEALISTIC CREATIVE ACTIVITY is the most wonderful way to use the God-given essence of life (reproductive seed), rather than through excessive sexual activity; this constructive conscious activity will also allow the preservation of the physical body.

IF AN INDIVIDUAL SEEKS THE LIGHT with one hand and the addictive pleasure of the senses with the other hand, they will not receive much light.

IF ASCENSION ENERGY GIFTED TO HUMANITY is not used for its ascension, it has the free will to be used for the opposite.

IF GIFTED LIFE ENERGY within the physical body is applied constructively, the result is joy, happiness and success; if the gifted energy is used destructively, the result is destruction.

IF THE ASCENSION STUDENT with committed, constant determination will receive and accept their I AM Presence, they will cause their consciousness (their vibratory rate) to be raised and will experience ascension first hand; all human failings will evaporate, and they will transmute into their light body.

"I HAVE COME TO CLAIM YOUR SOUL AND THE FIRES OF YOUR HEART FOR THE VICTORY OF THIS NEW AGE," Saint Germain.

IMAGE AND LIKENESS OF GOD is how humanity was imagined and created.

IN ALL THE UNIVERSE bless all forms of life and heal all human wounds and ego defenses that forget from whence you came.

IN SPITE OF NEGATIVE FORCES in the world, it is essential that the mastery student remain positive to attain mastery.

INCA people had an inner understanding and connection to higher realms; through their devotion they achieved great things.

INTERSTELLAR SPACE is filled with pure light consciousness; the great oceans of universal light exist throughout creation, manifesting form everywhere held together by love.

INVOCATION TO THE VIOLET FLAME: "In the name of the Great I AM, I call to beloved Saint Germain to saturate the world with wave upon wave of **violet** fire to infuse every particle of life, every man, woman and child on this planet in an auric field of **Violet Flame** to protect and to awaken them. I ask that this action be sustained until perfection is restored. And so be it."

IT IS HUMANITY'S MISSION to manifest the next golden age of enlightenment using the power and wisdom of the Ascended Masters; are you ready?

IT IS THE DETERMINATION OF THE ASCENDED MASTERS that "The Light" shall flood the Earth and all its peoples at this time, and whatever cannot tolerate The Light will leave. The Law of Life is the Law of Light where all density and confrontation will end; no matter how things appear in your present outside world, surrender to this truth forever more.

IT IS THE HAND OF GOD that rules the universe, gives without limit the gifts to infinity, protects without limit and is the master presence of all creation.

JEWEL IN THE HEART OF GOD is the beloved land of America that St. Germain has loved and guarded for centuries.

KNOWING THE DIFFERENCE BETWEEN DESIRE AND APPETITE is essential; the activity of desire is one of eternal growth and expansion; appetite is an accumulation of energy created by human emotions (feelings) through habits and patterns; the majority of individuals are controlled by their feelings.

LACK OF TRUST was the energy of the original fall of human consciousness and the demise of all past golden ages; time to surrender through trust to the higher realms here to support and love us; you can do this through your discernment and resonance.

LAND OF LIGHT is America long ago, and now she will rebirth into her spiritual heritage; nothing can prevent a destiny of great import to the nations of the world, creating equality, harmony and balance. We the Ascended Masters love and guard you.

LAW OF LIFE avoids the cosmic wheel of cause and effect and the need for reincarnation by seeking the God within and holding it.

LAW OF LOVE is perfection manifest; it expresses peace, joy and unconditional love of creation; through its emotion it creates mind; Love owns ALL THERE IS and asks nothing for itself because it is eternally self-creating.

LAW OF THE ASCENDED MASTERS states, they are pure, perfect all powerful beings who never make mistakes.

LAW OF THE INDIVIDUAL does not allow the Ascended Masters to interfere with human free will and choice except in periods where the cosmic cycle supersedes the individual. The planet has entered such an ascension cycle now where a great outpouring of light is entering.

LAW OF UNIVERSAL states that creation in form exists that God may have something to express love upon in action.

LEARNING THE HARD WAY has been the past learning tool of humanity, and it will get harder unless humanity makes other choices at this time through its free will; this requires the energy of trust and surrendering to it.

LEARNING TO DEMAND AND COMMAND universal life forces is completely normal for the Ascended Master, fixing consciousness with absolute certainty, knowing creative forces are for their use.

LIFE BECOMES SIMPLER the more you understand life and perfection; when you fill your feelings and thoughts with Divine Love, the struggle to survive life is over.

LIFE IS PERFECTION and contains all perfect manifestation within itself; the divine duty of the individual is to be a receiver that maintains and sustains the perfection of life.

LIFE IS PERPETUAL MOTION filled with constant new creations, a forever river of growth and expansion.

LIFE ITSELF NEVER STRUGGLES; what struggles is the human lack of consciousness that attempts to limit life; if humanity will just let life be, the natural result will be perfection.

LIFE SAYS TO HUMANITY, expand and grow and allow God power to pour greater and larger perfection into you forever more; humanity's resistance to this is creating the world you see now.

LIFE is the only presence, consciousness, intelligence and power that can act or ever did act.

LIFE'S LAW states, "Happiness cannot exist except when love is pouring out." In the outpouring life flows constantly; the first and greatest outpouring of our love belongs to the personal God power, God consciousness that enables existence.

LIGHT is substance, energy and luminosity all in one; this pure electronic light is what the eternal spiritual body is made of.

LIGHT is the supreme perfection and control of all things; focusing on and love of the light allows creation.

LIMITLESS CREATION AND SELF EMPOWERMENT are humanity's divine destiny and destination; by raising your frequency through your I AM Presence, you can produce all that you divinely desire; there is no other force but you that can determine what will come into your world; that's how powerful you are.

LOCALIZED CREATION is you designing and creating perfection in the world and sending that out into the universe.

LOVE SERVES because it is the nature of love to give; it does not give to get.

LOVE YOUR OWN DIVINTY every chance you can, releasing life and energy to enjoy all the gifts of life.

LOVING THE COSMIC LIGHT allows a natural flow of energy, putting God power first, balancing humanity's relation to and with life, creating perfection.

LUMINOUS ESSENCE OF CREATION overpowers whatever seeks to oppose it; the Ascended Master knows this and is one with this wisdom; humanity can also achieve this.

MAINTAINING A FEELING OF PEACE is essential within self-mastery, allowing the God-self presence to maintain and sustain itself. Mastery is a process of inside out, not outside in.

MAKING CONTACT WITH THE LIGHT is meeting your all-knowing omnipresence face to face.

MAKING CONTACT with an Ascended Master can only be done through enough love and healing of the personality; they are not present to solve personal problems; their entire effort is with the awakening of the God self within; to make contact you need to attune your human beingness and surrender to learning what you need to learn.

MANKIND NEEDS to rise from its own selfishness and trust and surrender to all that God and nature have freely given; then humanity can become worthy to be trusted with the treasures.

MANKIND for eons has qualified universal substance with lack and limitation, negative emotions, duality and separation; these have been returned to humanity through the planet's clearing and cleansing.

MANY COMMITTED PEOPLE being and doing constructive lives are often members of the Great White Brotherhood (bringing the Christ light into the world) before they become conscious of it.

MANY GREAT MASTERS have been working for the past hundred years into the present to protect and guard America, preparing wonders for the enlightenment of humanity and blessings untold to come and be shared in the world.

MANY PEOPLE BLAME LIFE for any pain or suffering they have endured, not knowing they are the creator creating all the time.

MASTER OF ALL THERE IS, past, present or future is Divine Love, an eternal, invincible presence of the I AM Presence.

MASTERING SELF is the mission of humanity; when this is achieved, everything else within the universe becomes a co-worker to manifest whatever the person wills through love.

MASTERS OF LOVE, LIGHT & WISDOM are the Ascended Masters; only through these once human beings, now Divine Beings, can humanity know the meaning of life and obtain ascension.

MASTERY OR ADEPTSHIP is achieved by knowing your God Self, having no doubt, stilling emotions and agreeing not to misuse power.

MASTERY is possible for every human being to attain and express right here, right now.

MEDITATION is needed for the communion with the Light of God within one's self, maintaining balance between your God self and the personal outer self.

MIRACLES are the result of the activation of the omnipresent cosmic law; when an individual knows and applies this law governing manifestation, they can produce intended results; thus, there are no miracles.

MIRACLES do not exist; all is according to Universal Law; it has to do with human present consciousness and application of law.

MORE WONDERS will be gifted to humanity as people ascend in conscious understanding and can accept the responsibility of these advancements, ascending into the next golden age.

MOST OF HUMANITY HOLDS A GREAT FEAR of their I AM Presence and embracing their divinity; feel the fear (an absence of love) anyway in order to release it; beyond the fear is love of your divinity waiting.

MOST OF HUMANITY has no idea or knowledge of the love and support the marvelous Ascended Masters constantly give humanity; they are the grand givers of all good.

MOVING IN CIRCLES is the motion of the universe; all things must return unto their Source; this is ascension.

NATURE IS CONSTANTLY reflecting back to humanity through "acts of God" how humanity treats nature; supported by the Ascended Masters, nature is stronger than humanity; thus, humanity's actions only harm itself; it is the destiny of humanity to live in complete cooperation with nature and for both to consciously support and love one another.

NEGATIVE FEELINGS & THOUGHTS rearrange the ratio and rate of speed of electrons within atoms, thus creating negative reality.

NEVER LOSE THE EXCITEMENT OF YOUR JOURNEY to love; accept and apply your I AM Presence. This is a vital reminder from beloved St. Germain.

NO FAILURE exists for anyone who continues to make self-conscious effort to express mastery of self; failure only comes when effort ceases.

NORTH AMERICA is to carry the Christ Light and be the way shower for the rest of the world; America is the heart center of the Final Golden Age.

NOTHING IN LIFE IS MORE IMPORTANT than you loving, accepting, appreciating and receiving your I AM Presence within yourself and the Universe.

NOTHING IN THE UNIVERSE GOES BACKWARD; no matter how anything appears, everything is moving forward to greater joy and perfection.

NOTHING is impossible.

NOW IS THE TIME for humanity to awaken to the all-empowering presence of God acting through each individual.

OBEDIENCE to the Eternal Laws of Love will release humanity from its struggle to survive life, allowing joy and perfection to abide forever more.

OH AMERCIA, you are the beloved children of light and way shower among nations leading to the incoming golden age.

ONE GREAT GOD is the Source of all happiness, eternity, pathway of light.

ONE GREAT PRINCIPLE OF CREATION is love that is the heart and Source of all and the hub upon which the spokes of existence are formed.

ONE SOURCE of all good is God.

ONLY BECAUSE OF A LACK OF LOVE do fear, doubt and ignorance exist on Earth; let the I AM Presence replace this.

ONLY BY BECOMING ONE with something or someone through feelings can you ever really know (anything).

ONLY BY RECEIVING from the all-knowing mind of God can you ever be its light.

ONLY FEAR, DOUBT AND IGNORANCE make mankind believe anything is impossible; ascension students accept an all-powerful Source of creation.

ONLY GOD is supreme.

ONLY MANKIND is guilty of making discord, for all else lives and acts in accordance with the Law of Love, Life, Harmony and Light.

ONLY ONE THING can manifest perfection in creation, and that is enough Divine Love; so love your personal I AM Presence unconditionally, so nothing else can come into your life or world.

ONLY THE CHRIST (in you) is eternal and real.

ONLY THE LIGHT is true.

ONLY WHEN DIVINE LOVE moves from the believing mental body to the knowing heart does it transmute from being a concept to a building block that can manifest anything.

ORIGINAL PURITY OF LIFE light energies are pouring into Earth at this time to clear and cleanse actions of the past and present to wake up and strengthen humanity evolving into the Final Golden Age.

PASSPORT TO HIGHER REALMS is through enough love poured into your Godself and to the higher realms; united the human discord and selfishness can vanish.

PEOPLE OF AMERICA awaken and know what freedom, power and light await your destiny through the use of the great loving presence.

PEOPLE WHO ONLY WANT THE AMUSEMENTS OF THE SENSES do not really want God; when people get sick and tired of being sick and tired perhaps they will choose the support of the higher realms.

PERFECT SELF CONTROL is never being surprised, disappointed or your feelings hurt under any circumstance.

PERFECTION AND DOMINION is God within the individual; this presence within the heart of everyone is the Source of life.

PERFECTION is achieved through self-correction of human weakness and full adoration of the Divine Being within.

PERFECTION takes no more energy than imperfection.

PERMANENT CONTACT with the great cosmic light, bringing a world of equality, harmony and balance through the great ones of love is the Earth's soul plan. During a new paradigm the human heart and head will receive constant conscious consideration and attention from higher realms.

PHYSICAL BODIES are the temples of the higher realms; through loving self you open to all possibilities and probabilities.

PHYSICAL INCARNATION is for the purpose of preparing, perfecting and infusing a body with the I AM Presence.

PLAN OF GOD is love, peace and perfection of creation.

POSITIVE FEELINGS AND THOUGHTS within the human mind and body are the activities of love and order, and they create comparable realties.

PRAYER NEEDS TO BE an outpouring of love and gratitude to the I AM Presence for the limitless chances and joyful things contained in life; often prayer is a "want list."

PRIMAL ATTRIBUTES OF LIFE are love, wisdom, and power to build eternal creation; when humanity heals its self-centered density, all life will express perfection.

PROJECTED CONSCIOUSNESS is complete consciousness and mastery over all your faculties every moment, increasing the rate of vibration of the atomic structure in your emotions, thoughts and physical body.

PROOF OF THE INNER GOD SELF has been experienced during past golden ages and will again be experienced by the present people of America.

PSYCHIC REALM FASCINATION over the eons has helped keep humanity in a childlike state, needing the wisdom and support of the Ascended Masters to raise human consciousness to adulthood in order to fully express life's full Divine Plan.

PURE DIVINE LOVE is the sacred key that unlocks the door of eternal freedom; there is no obstruction in Creation to this Love.

PURE ELECTRONIC LIGHT exists throughout creation; when the physical body becomes all light, it enters into the one eternal element from which God created all form; at this moment the condition of complete freedom is obtained.

PURE ELECTRONIC SUBSTANCE is the substance that fills infinity; all forms are created from this; this limitless substance everywhere is yours to mold without limit through your I AM Presence.

PURE UNIVERSAL SUBSTANCE OF GOD is being received within every moment of the now; it creates and generates and must be received back in mind and body, for all things in the universe move in circles.

PURIFYING POWER OF THE VIOLET FLAME can be achieved by visualizing yourself standing within a column of **Violet** Flame, flooding from toe to head and extending several feet on either side of your physical body; hold this for several moments allowing the purifying effect of God power to fill every atom of your body; this balances your emotional and mental bodies, allowing a balanced flow of energy throughout every cell in your body, raising your consciousness.

RADIATION OF ASCENDED MASTERS is the sustaining power they maintain.

RE-EMBODIMENT (REINCARNATION) is the activity in human evolution that gives self an opportunity to free yourself from yourself.

REALITY OF LIFE when truly understood allows all manifestations that seem miraculous to be normal.

REJECTION OF TRUTH does not make it so.

RELEASING negative feelings, thoughts and imperfect words creates freedom, acceptance and forgiveness for how a student has chosen to learn; this frees everyone; forgiveness fills all with light perfection.

REMEMBER, DIVINE LOVE IS an emoted feeling, an actual ray of Light that streams out from the heart flame; it is the most invincible power in the universe; use it without lack or limitation.

RETURN ALL POWER & AUTHORITY to the great, glorious God Flame, which is the real self and Source from all you have received.

RIGHT DESIRE is the purest form of prayer.

RIGHT TO RULE is achieved when humanity learns to obey the rules of creation; when this is achieved all creation will obey humanity also.

SACRED FIRE is the way humanity forgives all mistakes of itself, forgiving all that is not love.

SAINT GERMAIN'S GLOSSARY, Ascended Masters' Teachings, Terms & Tools, is a simplified, concise reference to readily reveal to each one the destination of their Divine Self, so it may be shared with the world. This glossary honors all that has preceded it and the value of that detailed teaching.

SECOND STEP IN CREATION is to state your plan in words as clearly as you can; write this down.

SEEKING THE LIGHT is always known to the Ascended Masters.

SELF EFFORT of the individual is the only way mastery can be achieved; the intention of the Ascended Masters is to lead all of humanity to their mastery through mastering the self (a reflection of ALL THERE IS).

SELF PITY is the pinnacle of human selfishness; through self-pity the personal consciousness absorbs pity into the desires of the physical body; the I AM Presence is abandoned; its divine energy is then used in non-constructive endeavors.

SELF-CONSCIOUSNESS OF LIFE is you experiencing you.

SELF-CONSCIOUS APPLICATION is when humanity understands they can only receive that for which an effort is made and then God-dominion begins.

SELFISHNESS and misuse of transcendent wisdom and power were the cause of the demise of all past golden ages.

SELFISHNESS and the need for power to control others blinds reason, prevents spirituality; you cannot control what you did not create.

SEND YOUR LOVE BACK TO YOUR I AM PRESENCE, and ask it to give you what it wants you to have; it gives you the very breath you breathe.

SENSE CONSCIOUS man became instead of God conscious and manifested what he thought upon, creating lack and limitation.

SEPARATION FROM GOD begins to express itself in your body and world, causing one to feel apart from creation; once separate from God, intelligence and power have a beginning and an end.

SERUMS MADE FROM ANIMALS do not serve the highest good of humanity nor truly assist in the well-being of anyone; these destructive actions destroy the ideals of humanity.

SERVING is allowing your mind and body through God's power to act as a channel.

SIGHT AND HEARING are aspects of the same activity; sound contains color and color contains sounds; when still enough you can experience this.

SIMILARITY creates oneness through cause and effect.

SO-CALLED DEATH is an opportunity for rest, reflection and attunement of personal consciousness, a respite from the chaos of Earth in order to receive light and energy in order to experience another physical incarnation.

SON OF URIEL was once in a past life the name of Saint Germain during an incarnation.

SOURCE OF ALL LIFE is attained through loving obedience, purity and Divine Love to each one's God Self-Presence.

SOURCE OF LIFE is the giver of every good and perfect thing; attention to Source is the golden key to every good thing.

STAYING CONNECTED TO YOUR I AM PRESENCE allows you to always be God directed, being invincible, never failing.

SUBSTANCES THAT NEED TO BE CLEARED FROM THE BODY which impede the ascension processes of humanity are (in order of the toxicity): narcotics, alcohol, meat, tobacco, excess sugar, salt and strong coffee. Calling on your I AM Presence will eliminate pain or suffering in the non-use or reduced use of these substances; these substances contain a dense energy that keeps you anchored within a lower vibration.

SUPERHUMAN LOVE achieves all extraordinary accomplishments through wisdom and power from an Ascended Master.

SUPERNATURAL conditions do not exist in the universe; all that is transcendent and perfect is natural and reflects the Law of Love; other than this is sub-natural.

SUPREME PRESENCE is the great flame of Love and Light.

THE ALL-KNOWING is where all patterns of perfection are stored in the I AM Presence and manifested through the will of the person.

THE ALMIGHTY COMMAND OF CREATION is: "Be yea perfect, even as your father in heaven is perfect." Life will return to you, in individuated consciousness, multiple times through human incarnations until you master your ascension process.

THE ASCENDED MASTER CONSCIOUSNESS is fully and constantly committing to receive and accept the I AM Presence, so their consciousness, their vibratory rate, rises, and all human failings evaporate, and they transmute into their light body.

THE ASCENDED MASTER CONSCIOUSNESS is the only I AM Presence that can assist humanity in re-establishing balance and peace upon the Earth; only its Flame of Divine Love can dissolve all fear, doubt and ignorance, the monsters of mankind.

THE ASCENDED MASTER CONSCIOUSNESS never encumbers itself with the density/baggage of humanity; within the higher realms pure substance is applied to manifest divine desire through picturing and visualizing form.

THE ASCENDED MASTER is a person who, by a self-conscious personal process effort, has manifested enough inner love and power to break the chains of all human lack and limitation, stands free and worthy to be trusted with the universal forces of creation, controlling all by the energetic manipulation of the Light and Love within.

THE ASCENDED MASTERS' WAY OF LIFE is to give, first and foremost, love and gratitude to their I AM Presence and then expand love and perfection to all.

THE ASCENDED MASTER'S DETERMINATION is love, wisdom, power, illumination and comprehension, moving from darkness to light, freeing you from those who attempt to control what they did not create, to know the truth from the untruth, to free you from the unhealed self.

THE ASCENSION ASPIRANT is cutting off forever the destructive activities of the animal nature in man, allowing the soul to transmute into its complete divine activity united with the perfection of Source.

THE ASCENSION STUDENT must master their feeling body by controlling it through love, wisdom and the self-empowerment of their I AM Presence; the majority of individuals are controlled by their feelings.

THE ASTRAL/PSYCHIC REALM contains only the disembodied human creations fostered by negative feelings, thoughts, words and actions of personal consciousness; there is no wisdom within this frequency; the Ascended Masters are intending to receive a dispensation to free us from this fourth dimensional realm, since it has slowed humanity's growth.

THE ATOM is a breathing, living being created by the love of God through the intention of self-conscious intelligence by feelings and thoughts.

THE ATOM IS PURE SPIRIT or Light of God remaining eternally perfect.

THE ATOMIC ACCELERATOR is an ascension device where the vibratory action of the physical atom is raised until it becomes pure electronic essence/spirit; the perfected body becomes eternally youthful, beautiful and powerful; in this state, the ascended person can function wherever they choose with no time or space barriers.

THE AVERAGE PERSON lives life after life without once loving or thanking their own I AM Presence for the energy that maintains and sustains their life or the joy of being alive; even a tiny bit of gratitude and love to their I AM Presence would transmute all negativity.

THE AVERAGE PERSON'S FEELING AND THOUGHTS are reflections of their wounds and ego defenses filled with negative, chaotic, unloving energy, reflecting the world around them; harmony, love, balance and peace are the connecting power of the universe; these appear from within your I AM Presence, your God Self.

THE BELOVED MIGHTY I AM PRESENCE is the only Source which knows all that is required to build patterns of creation that produce perfection.

THE CENTRAL POINT OF LIFE is light energy within every atom, composing the substance from which all physical life comes.

THE CHECKING ACCOUNT OF LIFE AND THE BANK OF THE UNIVERSE is Divine Love; it instantly draws all good things into life; all activity becomes joy and perfection with your withdrawal.

THE CHOOSER is you decreeing the qualities and form you intend to pour into life with no fear, doubt or ignorance.

THE CHRIST CONSCIOUSNESS is the only consciousness in creation that can say "I AM."

THE CHRIST MIND is embodied in great beings on the sun; God sent forth his rays individualizing itself in order to direct through self-conscious human beings; this is the reason humans are the sons of God gifted with free will.

THE COHESIVE POWER of the universe is love; without it the universe would not exist.

THE CONSCIOUSNESS OF GOD is the guardian of all through its Love and Power until that which is human can no longer misuse and abuse life.

THE CONSERVATION OF LIFE ESSENCE, reproductive energy, is the most powerful tool toward ascension; using it in combination with the I AM Presence and controlling emotions and thoughts is a clear pathway to perfection.

THE CORE OF LOVE is like the magnetic poles of the Earth or the heart and spine of the physical body.

THE COSMIC ACTIVITY AND LIGHT from planet Earth is expanding and growing constantly; many are feeling this increased energy; it is time to apply this new energy in a constructive ascension process.

THE COSMIC MIRROR sees the complete series of lifetimes, the cause and effect of choices, consciousness and how often the incarnational process of mastery is learned.

THE DELUSIONS OF PYSCHIC SUGGESTIONS do not contain any I AM Presence nor wisdom to assist humanity to free itself from itself; no one but an Ascended being can know what has been in the past of un-ascended humanity.

THE DOER, THE DOING AND THE DEED is God manifesting.

THE EARLY AMERICAN PATRIOTS were given the inspiration as to how to build a nation of God's freedom by the Ascended Masters, so a nation of freedom would lead the world into freedom.

THE EARTH IS EXPERIENCING THE BIRTH OF A NEW PARADIGM no matter how things appear in the outside world; things are changing through cosmic consciousness energies coming in, realizing war does not work, shifting hatred to love and from me consciousness to we consciousness, living by the Law of Love.

THE EMOTIONAL BODY is the receptive feminine activity of consciousness; the mental body is the assertive masculine activity; a thought never becomes actualized until it passes through the emotional body; feelings and thoughts are creating human reality all the time.

THE EMOTIONAL BODY, the feelings of humanity, is a powerful container of energy; feelings create thoughts; emotions and thoughts together create reality; through the conscious knowledge and control of emotions and thoughts new realities can be created; the lack of knowing this has created great suffering throughout the history of humanity.

THE ETERNAL BIRTHRIGHT of every human being is to awaken their divinity through the journey of the human experience.

THE ETERNAL MOTTO of the Ascended Master is "to know, to dare, to do, and to be silent."

THE EVOLUTION OF EVERY PLANET comes to a point where full expression of its Divine Soul Plan must be experienced; for Earth it is learning to love, creating a world of equality, harmony and balance; this moment has come for planet Earth.

THE FALL OF MAN is the deliberate choice of an imperfection, a condition less than God.

THE FIRE ELEMENT, working in conjunction with the human body to consume energetic imbalances, often produces the feeling of pain if the personality is in resistance, but if the person is in acceptance the feeling of peace is achieved.

THE FIRST INTENTION OF CREATION that went into infinity was, "Let there be light," and then creation happened; out of the primal light comes all manifested form.

THE FOLLY OF HUMANITY is wasting or abusing nature's gifts.

THE FOLLY OF MANKIND can no longer continue its insane destructive feelings and survive; the ascension time is upon the planet and humanity; it is time to learn the way of the light during this final ascension process of the planet.

THE FULL ACCEPTANCE of the I AM Presence governs all life in complete balance.

THE GIVER AND DOER of all good in the world is through the God within human hearts.

THE GOD CONSCIOUSNESS within us cannot grieve; humanity is learning no one leaves this universe; know when someone leaves this frequency, they have gone to a higher frequency better than the one they left.

THE GOD IN YOU is always directing and is the master of every moment of now.

THE GRATIFICATION OF HUMAN APPETITE and satisfaction of the senses can only result in addictive destruction and unhappiness.

THE GREAT CENTRAL SUN is a definite place in space; its almighty life sustains all in this Milky Way galaxy, sustaining all solar systems; it is a universal presence, invincible power and eternal love.

THE GREAT COSMIC WHEEL OF PROGRESS affects the entire planet, governing the expansion of light operating the complete system; it will negate the destructive human forces and awaken them to the power greater than selfish human behavior.

THE GREAT CREATIVE WORDS are "I AM".

THE GREAT ENERGY OF LIFE is constantly charging through humanity; what you do with it is your choice.

THE GREAT FIRE BREATH is a constant outpouring of Divine Love; its three attributes are love, wisdom and power in action.

THE GREAT GOD ENERGY WITHIN is radiated into the personal self by the great God self.

THE HEART OF GOD is ever expanding, ever perfect form and home of Divine Love, Light, Wisdom and Power; this is the heart center of manifested form.

THE HEART OF INFINITY is Divine Love that lives within the heart of each individual; this is an ever releasing, unlimited energy of wisdom, power and substance.

THE HUMAN BODY is God's temple of energy, which the great God presence provides and intends to express by activation of its soul plan purpose to be here. If human habits waste this energy, the energy is steadily withdrawn and physical death occurs.

THE HUMAN BODY is always under the conscious control of the will and choices of the person occupying it. Everything that happens to the body is and will always be under the control of the person's free will.

THE HUMAN PERSONALTY when not obedient to its I AM Presence is an imbalanced being in creation.

THE HUMAN RACE CANNOT BE HEALED by itself; the I AM Presence has maintained and sustained humanity for eons and is now a vital force within the ascension process of the planet and humanity.

THE INDIVIDUAL SELF actually owns nothing; all has been loaned to it from the beings of creation; no matter how much misuse of the divine gifts of life are expressed, you are loved and supported until you awake.

THE INFINITE ACTS AND CONTROLS THE UNIVERSE through its own individualization, through higher beings who state, "I AM"; creation could have not taken place if the infinite had not acknowledged its own being through the "Individual I AM." This may be challenging for the human mind to comprehend at present, but soon you will learn to think with your heart and know this truth.

THE INNER LIGHT will never fail unless the ascension student turns it off.

THE JEWEL OF MY HEART is how Saint Germain refers to America, leading the world into another golden age.

THE LAST HURDLE, DEATH, will not be needed anymore and will disappear when humanity is ready to embrace the perfect activity and joy of life.

THE LAW OF BEING allows the individual to use their own energy through an emotion, thought and word to become an action in manifestation.

THE LAW OF CAUSE & EFFECT, the law governing all form, will tolerate humanity's injustice to humanity only so long; when the intent to do harm is directed to the Source of life, there is an automatic balancing process in all life.

THE LAW OF LIFE is heaven, peace, harmony and love to every created thing; all seen and unseen things in creation employ this law; humanity is the only creature on Earth that creates the opposite of this law.

THE LAW OF LIFE is to give; for only by giving of one 's self can you grow and expand; to give the mighty love of your I AM Presence into world service, employing Divine Love which permeates everything; this giving will create a balance of giving and receiving.

THE LAW OF ONE knows there is no opposite; God desiring, God feeling, God knowing, God manifesting and God controlling all.

THE LAW OF PERFECTION states, "Whatever negative feelings or thoughts are thrust out into the world by an individual, it will vibrate through the mental and physical bodies of the sender before it can reach the receiver and the rest of the universe."

THE LAW OF PHYSICAL INCARNATION states, when life essence (reproductive energy) is used beyond creating another human being in sexual excesses, the disintegration of the physical body begins; this is the principal reason for physical death with human beings.

THE LAW OF THE CIRCLE is the remaining mastery of humanity within the ascension process, knowing all things return to their Source through the motion of the circle; when this is mastered all discord on Earth will cease.

THE LAW OF THE ETERNAL states: "The light of God never fails."

THE LIFE in every person is God; only through self-conscious effort can the riches of good manifest and discord be removed.

THE LIGHT IS ALWAYS DIRECTED BY FEELINGS AND THOUGHTS; it is essential that all students learn to control and direct all three; conscious control is how the Ascended Masters accomplish seemingly impossible results.

THE LIGHT OF GOD NEVER FAILS.

THE LIGHT does not accept imbalance into it; as the student transmutes into the Light, they become the Light.

THE MAGIC KEY unlocks God power when the feeling of peace and unconditional love to every person and everything is held in place; holding love and serenity in the personal self allows the God presence to act in every moment.

THE MAGIC PRESENCE is another book where Saint Germain shares more experiences and wisdom with humanity.

THE MAGIC PRESENCE is the I AM; humanity's I AM Presence resides within the etheric body of every person some ten to sixty feet above the physical body; it lives in its own higher realm frequency forever expanding itself through the individual.

THE MASS OF HUMANITY seeks the possession and ownership of things that they can never truly own, which is an inversion of the Law of Life.

THE MASTER CHRIST within human hearts is the I AM Presence.

THE MASTER RECORD OF HUMANITY was what humanity was modeled from in the beginning of time, a perfect being, an Ascended Master in the image and likeness of God through the I AM Presence.

THE MASTERY STUDENT is in the process of learning how to maintain and sustain the I AM Presence in order to release Divine Love, Light and Power; at present, the ability to comprehend this is increasing through the ascension process of the planet itself.

THE MIGHTY GOD SELF within you is the supreme ruler of all creation and the only dependable, permanent eternal Source of help in existence.

THE MIGHTY I AM PRESENCE is also known as the owner and doer of all that is good.

THE MOST ESSENTIAL ACTIVITY OF LIFE is love, devotion and gratitude for all the diversity of life and what it teaches.

THE MOST INVINCIBLE POWER IN THE UNIVERSE is Divine Love without limit, making nothing impossible.

THE MOST POWERFUL ENERGY IN THE UNIVERSE, the life force, creates all worlds; this energy is given to humanity to attain their ascension; if this energy is not used for ascension, it has the free will to be used for the opposite.

THE ONE GREAT SELF is the life energy that knows there is only one power that can ever accomplish any good thing directing all constructive activities, and that is Divine Love.

THE ONE LAW OF LIFE is love, harmony and peace.

THE ONE LAW OF LIFE is love.

THE ONE exists and controls everything in creation.

THE ONE is the God, the Christ, the Light; all else is shadow.

THE ONLY EVIL ON EARTH is the one humanity has created, most done through fear, doubt and ignorance; often this evil is caused by people who consciously made a choice to do so; if you destroy, you will be destroyed is cosmic law.

THE ONLY TRUE SERVICE is to consciously use the energy of God within for the good of all, always.

THE OUTER HUMAN PART is what is called the personality, the vehicle through which perfection is expressed into the outer world and universe.

THE PERFECT PLAN only exists within the I AM Presence; when the emotional and mental bodies are illuminated by this presence, perfection becomes possible.

THE PERSONAL SELF is often claiming things and power when the energy by which self-exists is loaned by the God-Self.

THE PHYSICAL BODY, the actual atomic structure of matter, is the densest form of creation and is the result of emotions and thoughts; formlessness is the Eternal True Form of all that you will return to.

THE PSYCHIC REALM fascinates and entertains some people; the Ascended Masters explain there is nothing supportive nor instructive from the psychic realm; it is the creation of the human sense consciousness containing an accumulation of human feelings and thoughts; there is none of the Christ Consciousness or Cosmic Light Energies present.

THE PURPOSE OF THIS GLOSSARY is to present simplified, concise ascension terminology that the average person can quickly understand during these times of change and chaos.

THE RADIATION FROM GOLD has a powerful purifying and energizing effect within the human body and throughout nature; during past golden ages, gold was used as a spiritual tool; gold was never meant to be hoarded.

THE REAL YOU is a glorious angelic being and power who is always pouring its energy into your God Individualized Self.

THE REALITY OF DEATH is a powerful reminder to humanity of its disobedience to the original God plan; death is the last hurdle for humanity to conquer by reconnecting with the divine way of life; then humanity returns to its Eternal Divine Self.

THE REASON MOST HUMANS DIE is because of the waste of electronic light through emotional excesses; the waste of life energy through uncontrolled feelings is the cause and effect of the disintegration of the physical body; others die through some form of violence.

THE SAME OPPORTUNITY is available to everyone who commits enough attention and intention to their ascension through the eternal I AM Presence.

THE SECRET TO ASCENDED MASTERS' SUPREME AUHORITY comes in knowing that Divine Love is a presence, intelligence, a principle, a light, a power, an activity and a substance; there is no one and no thing that can obstruct the approach of Divine Love anywhere in creation.

THE SECRET within the human ascension process is to keep constant (inner) communication with the I AM Presence so that its perfection is transferred to the world and may assist in purifying and healing humanity.

THE SPIRITUAL PROGRESS AND HEART CENTER of the Earth is America; the foundation of the Christ Consciousness for humanity lies in the creation of America; America carries the light of the Cosmic Christ that will illuminate the planet into equality, harmony and balance.

THE STATUE OF LIBERTY is a focus of spiritual power guarding America; the torch represents the Light of the I AM Presence sending peace and love to all humanity; the feminine form itself is a representation of the great presence which carries the Cosmic Light for all of humanity.

THE STUDENT OF LIGHT knows not to judge, shame or blame any human limitations as an aspect to their ascension; to do so would hold them in place and prevent their freedom.

THE SUN IN THIS SOLAR SYSTEM is to the whole solar system what the heart is to the human body; its currents of energy being the blood stream of this system of planets. The ether belt around Earth is the 'lungs' through which the currents of energy continually flow, cleansing the body of Earth; the sun is also the head of this solar system through which this cosmic energy constantly generates via the responsibility of Ascended Master activity.

THE SUN IS NOT HOT; it is cool and becomes hot when the sun's currents of electronic energy pass through the atmosphere of the Earth; the sun is the electronic pole and the Earth the magnetic pole; the atmosphere is the element through which the currents diversify.

THE SUN is a container of constructively gathered energy and substance created for human use.

THE SUPREME GOD PRESENCE loans the very atoms of the body to humanity from the great sea of universal substance.

THE TEMPLE OF THE I AM PRESENCE is the physical body, the life energy which moves humanity through life, allowing humanity to be God in action.

THE TERM, ELECTRON, means an eternally pure heart center of immortal fire, a perfect balance of light (science calls it a force field); the electron is eternally perfect; the force field is subject to expansion and contraction; this is the determining factor in bringing substance into form from the invisible to visible.

THE TERM, SELF-CONSCIOUS, means the individual who is conscious of their Source and perfection of life expressing through themselves.

THE TRUE MEANING OF ASCENSION is returning to Source; all things in the universe move in circles; this is what is happening to Earth and humanity now.

THE TRUE MEANING OF FRIENDSHIP is when you transcend from me consciousness to we consciousness, an ascended state of being one, being unconditional love, the most loving relationship in the universe.

THE TRUE STUDENT OF ASCENSION does not use their 5D wisdom or powers for the validation and gratification of their human senses or for producing income through 4D psychic/astral means.

THE VIOLET FLAME is a vital tool for spiritual progress and evolution, offering forgiveness and compassion, creating harmony and balance; the flame dissolves karma; it will not get rid of something but will assist in balancing it, teaching lessons you need to learn in a loving, gentle manner.

THE WILL of a person is supreme over the body temple; everyone leaves their body by willing it so.

THE WORD IS MADE FLESH by the living, breathing atom being brought into existence by the love of God and self-conscious intelligence fueled by feelings and thoughts.

THE WORD OF GOD is how all creation manifests, and without this creation does not happen; there is only one power than can move through creation and that is the magnificent electronic light existing everywhere, all the time, flooding through all manifestations.

THE WORDS "I AM" whether felt, thought or spoken, release the power of creation automatically.

THE WORK OF ASCENDED MASTER MESSENGERS is to tell the truth, and the truth will set you free from fear, doubt and ignorance.

THE WORLD AT LARGE is an unsettling place filled with those who think they can control what they did not create, killing those who disagree with them; this reality needs to be redeemed and saved from its own destruction; assisting in the saving of humanity is a major role of the Ascended Masters.

THERE ARE NO ACCIDENTS or chance anywhere within the universe; all is in Divine Order.

THERE IS A COSMIC LAW that states, whatever you are conscious of in feelings and thoughts you imprint all around you; your consciousness creates your reality all the time.

THERE IS NO STRONGER LOVE in the universe than that between an Ascended Master and their student.

THERE IS ONLY ONE FOUNDATION upon which permanent happiness, freedom and perfection can be achieved; this is through the I AM Presence, releasing humanity from its wounds and ego defenses, deceit, denial of the deceit and greed.

THINKING OF A DEAD LOVED ONE joins you with the loved one by joining in consciousness; mastering this truth eliminates much suffering in the world.

THINKING draws upon itself.

THIRD STEP IN CREATION is to close your eyes and see within your mind a mental picture of the desired finished plan.

THOUGHTS AND FEELINGS are living, vibrating things; those who know this will use their wisdom and control them accordingly.

THRESHOLD OF THE AGES is upon the Earth where physical limitation and conflict will vanish like an old healed wound, no matter how the present outside world appears.

THROUGH DIVINITY, not anywhere else, is the pathway to ascension via Divine Love, divine feelings, divine thoughts, divine actions and divine ideals.

THROUGH HUMAN CONSCIOUSNESS every person can, if they so choose, release the unlimited power of the I AM Presence.

THROUGH LOVING YOUR GOD PRESENCE, as a student of life, the struggle to survive life stops.

THROUGH THE PRESENCE OF GOD mankind never stops being the creator creating; this also allows corrections of mis-creations.

THROUGH THE SPOKEN WORD, following the emotion and thought, manifestation of form comes into the world.

THROUGHOUT THE EARTH there are many quickly awakening and feeling the rush of Inner Light pouring into them, cutting off the imbalanced creation of the outer world, allowing the mighty creator of the universe to prevail.

THROUGHOUT THE UNIVERSE all knowledge and wisdom are open to self-conscious, good-willed persons who wish to understand the cosmos and all reality.

TO COME IN CONTACT WITH AN ASCENDED MASTER is to think upon them, call unto them, and they will answer every call if the motive is love of one Source, love of Light and love of Perfection.

TO CREATE POSITIVE CHANGE is the alchemical energy of the **Violet Flame**, a combination of powerful blue and loving pink, balancing masculine and feminine energies; all can be forgiven and transmuted through this flame; it dissolves imbalances in the auric field and consciousness.

TO LOVE AND BLESS LIFE in all its diversified forms, let this be your code of honor: all life has a divine birthright to be here; this is the eternal plan of existence.

TO MANIFEST THE EXPRESSIONS OF THE I AM PRESENCE, intently become aware of that presence within yourself; know that your very life energy comes from this Source, the heart center of the cosmic life of creation.

TRANSCENDENT and MAGNIFICENT ACTIVITIES of Love and Light are the natural conditions God used to create humanity learning to love.

TRANSMUTING NEGATIVE FEELINGS and thoughts in your emotional and mental bodies is a powerful use of the **Violet Flame**, healing the core unhealed energies causing pain and suffering in life.

TRUTH OF LIFE is when you accept the Mighty God Presence within your own being.

TURN WITHIN TO YOUR MIGHTY MASTER; this will enable you to know your I AM Presence; this will allow the Ascended Master wisdom to manifest directly into your life stream, healing all wounds and ego defenses by infusing your feelings with Divine Love.

TWO ASCENDED MASTER REQUIREMENTS are, first, a person need connect with their own divinity, God, I AM Presence, and constantly focus that out into the world; second, a person need balance their feelings through Divine Love as a force blessing everyone and everything. To the person who is and does these things unlimited higher realm assistance is available.

TWO GREAT CENTERS OF LIGHT are presently pouring blessings to humanity: one is the higher realm presence of Shamballa and the other will appear in the United States of America (USA), the new JerUSAlem.

UNASCENDED INDIVIDUALS live in a vault of their own feelings and thoughts, and what they see in others is a reflection of their own delusion and creation, a reflection of their relationship with themselves.

UNBRIDLED SELFISHNESS healed will bless the entire world and create equality, harmony and balance.

UNIVERSAL SUBSTANCE obeys without exception the direction of emotions and thought and records through the emotional body of humanity; it is obedient to conscious will all the time.

UNIVERSAL SUPPLY is life itself existing everywhere.

UNIVERSAL/COSMIC LAW is unerring; you cannot receive without giving, and you cannot give without receiving; thus, the balance of life is maintained and sustained.

UNTIL HUMANITY UNDERSTANDS AND APPLIES the need to self-control their feelings through awakened consciousness, it is impossible to maintain and sustain a positive, permanent path forward; the feeling of Divine Love must move from a temporary thought to a permanent, perfected application.

UNVEILED MYSTERIES is a book in which Saint Germain revealed many sacred secrets to humanity.

USING YOUR TALENTS AND GIFTS is the fulfilling of the great universal Law of Service.

USE YOUR UNDERSTANDING OF THE I AM PRESENCE to bless all life everywhere, and more and more ascended wisdoms and powers will come forth.

VIOLET FLAME main God qualities and actions are: freedom, transmutation, transformation, diplomacy, ceremony and application of the science of true alchemy (healing self); invoke daily to release emotional, mental, etheric and physical imbalances; it is a combination of blue and pink light, blue for power and pink for love, balancing the energies of the divine masculine and feminine to create positive change.

WAY OF MASTERY is when we know our blessings are the result of the sustaining higher power giving it.

WE ASCENDED MASTERS are always free to use pure universal substance (with no intention to harm) for whatever purpose we choose and give it any specific quality we desire for the required task at hand.

WESTERN WORLD temperament is often sensitive, emotional and impulsive; until "waste of energy" is governed, permanent progress cannot be achieved.

WHAT CAUSES DEATH is the lack of Divine Light within the nervous system; the Light radiates life-essence which bonds the atoms together; that creates the physical body; the Light is owned by and comes from your I AM Presence.

WHAT HUMANITY CALLS MIRACLES are only the expression of universal laws; because of the perfection of these laws, the limitations of humanity are not included.

WHAT IS HELD IN CONSCIOUSNESS you bring into existence; this is how powerful you are; it is impossible for your life not to contain anything that is not your past or present accumulated consciousness; this is imprinted upon universal substance and brings forth like kind.

WHAT IS TRUE SERVICE? Many actions of individuals are gratifications of the human self, as their concepts of human's service to humans are often enslavements filled with lack and limitation of the God-self; true spiritual service is embracing the God-self, the master, within the human self; in focusing on human to human service, if an individual fails to fix upon the Source of all of love, it is not true service.

WHEN FORGIVENESS (acceptance + compassion) is true, a weight is lifted off the individual and the world. Peaceful joy returns; the forgiveness must also be truly forgotten to fully release yourself; by remembering, it continues to hold it in place.

WHEN LIFE ESSENCE (reproductive energy) is primarily used for sexual pleasure rather than creating another human being, the disintegration of the physical body begins; this is the inevitable, inexorable law of physical incarnation.

WHEN LIFE IS LIVED AS INTENDED, peace, love, equality and joy will replace the opposite of these; humanity has the strength to manifest these intentions and receive all the marvelous gifts of life.

WHEN RULING A NATION and you turn away from the forces of creation, God, it means the ultimate end to that government; a cosmic activity enters the planet which destroys them.

WHEN THE STUDENT knows how to bring forth the power of Divine Love from within their own I AM Presence at any moment, then they know their ascension is at hand.

WISDOM is the right use of all that manifests; when you know this truth all good in creation comes.

WITHIN THE ASCENDED STATE, every conceivable thing can be manifested.

WITHIN THE CENTER OF THE EARTH beyond the fire crust, there are ascended civilizations that have advanced through many cycles of self-mastery; they are assisting humanity as well with your ascension process; why should there not be life in the center as well as the surface of this planet? There is more to this world than you ever imagined.

WONDERS TO COME unlike anything ever known will come into use as the incoming golden age approaches.

WONDERS will be revealed more and more that all things are possible as you live in love and recognize your divinity; more marvelous inventions await you as you enter the golden crystal age.

WORKING TWENTY-FOUR SEVEN is your I AM Presence flowing through your emotions, thoughts and physical body, creating Divine Love, wisdom and power.

YELLOWSTONE NATIONAL PARK is named for the magnificent yellow diamonds found there.

YOU ARE A DIVINE BEING IN AN INCARNATED EXPERIENCE; can you accept with compassion and embrace this truth and forgive yourself for not doing so?

YOU ARE ALL children of God, a receiver of all good.

YOU ARE HERE to understand how to release the latent mighty God power within you; then anything will be possible.

YOU ARE THE DIRECTOR OF YOUR CONSCIOUSNESS by choosing which screenplay you wish to produce; if you do not like old choices, make another choice through your free will and I AM Presence.

YOU ARE WHAT YOUR ATTENTION AND INTENTION FOCUS UPON; most of humanity would not live beyond midlife if it were not for the constant love and support of ascended beings.

YOU BECOME A TRUE MESSENGER of divine service when the glorious God, I AM Presence, is fully accepted, embraced and shared with all.

YOU BECOME that upon which you meditate.

YOU CAN BE FREE by acknowledging and accepting the presence of the one mighty God anchored within the human heart and mind and knowing there is no room for anything else.

YOUR BELOVED SAINT GERMAIN has worked throughout the centuries to purify humanity's desire world; if America is to be purified, the people first must be; higher realms cannot protect that which is not pure; evil is a constant accumulation of disqualified energy that gratifies the senses until it results in physical death.

YOUR GLORIOUS SELF stands ever waiting for you.

YOUR LACK OF CONSCIOUSNESS has been a major obstacle to your ascension; time to wake up and release the erroneous beliefs from the past and present; this requires commitment to the process and doing the work.

YOUR PHYSICAL BODY is the vehicle upon and through which you can choose to let the I AM Presence enter, experiencing no human lack or limitation.

YOUR SOURCE is your beloved, eternal I AM Presence.

BEYOND YOUR UNHEALED SELVES,
THERE IS A HIGHER DIMENSION
WHERE YOU HAVE HEALED AND MASTERED SELF.
I SHALL MEET YOU THERE.

Your teacher & friend,
St Germain

ABOUT THE AUTHORS

St. GERMAIN

St Germain is the great Ascended Master who is serving as the guardian of mankind during humanity's new 2000-year Aquarian age, which began December 2012—as Jesus served as humanity's guide in the last 2,000-year age of Pisces. St Germain was a key force in the founding of the United States of America as a sanctuary for freedom and equality. His many incarnations on Earth have included Joseph, the husband of Mary, mother of Jesus; Merlin during the court of King Arthur; Christopher Columbus, who re-discovered North America; and Francis Bacon whom, he tells us, was the literary master we know as William Shakespeare. During his last human lifetime as the Count Saint Germain in France, St Germain inspired the creation of the United States of America.

JOEL D. ANASTASI

Phillip channeled all the wisdom contained in this work, a good deal of which Joel recorded and transcribed from his public and private conversations with St Germain, which the Angel News Network is publishing separately as *Divine Dialogues with St Germain*. Joel has been a news reporter, magazine editor, an officer in a major financial services company and a management consultant. He is the author of *The Second Coming* which records his interviews with Archangel Gabriel through channel Robert Baker. He created a human development program called *Life Mastery* based on teachings of the Archangel Michael channeled by Jeff Fasano. Joel's collaboration with channel Jessie Keener produced *The Ascension Handbook* by the Two Marys, the combined energies of Mary, the mother of Jesus, and Mary Magdalene, Jesus' twin flame. Joel holds a BS degree in economics from Syracuse University and an MS degree from the Columbia Graduate School of Journalism.

PHILLIP ELTON COLLINS

Phillip enjoyed careers in advertising and commercial film production which gave him opportunities to collaborate with many of the talented, rich and famous around the world. His advertising career began with Young & Rubicam in New York City. While still a relative youngster, he founded Fairbanks Films with film directors Ridley and Tony Scott, among others. Together they created a body of award-winning commercials that are still recognized today. Phillip moved to Lucas Films as Director of Marketing for Industrial Light and Magic (ILM), where he produced more award-winning commercials and helped pioneer the adaptation of feature film visual effects to advertising commercials. After years of spiritual studies, Phillip retired from commercial film production and began teaching and channeling higher realm entities, which has led to his publishing twelve books, including *The Refounding of America*.

Both Joel and Phillip feel honored and humbled by the opportunity to work with St Germain to bring this empowering message of creation to the world.

REFERENCES

ACTIVATE YOUR SOUL PLAN ! Angel Answers & Actions, by Phillip Elton Collins https://phillipeltoncollins.com/books/activate-your-soul-plan-angel-answers-actions/

A DEEPER UNDERSTANDING OF HUMAN LIFE, by Phillip Elton Collins https://phillipeltoncollins.com/deeper-understanding-of-human-life/

Angel News Network's CURRENT EVENTS BROADCASTING http://theangelnewsnetwork.com/category/podcast/current-events-broadcasting/

COMING HOME TO LEMURIA, AN ASCENSION ADVENTURE STORY, by Phillip Elton Collins https://phillipeltoncollins.com/books/coming-home-to-lemuria-an-ascension-adventure-story/

CREATING A WORLD OF LOVE, PEACE, EQUALITY, HARMONY & BALANCE, by Phillip Elton Collins https://phillipeltoncollins.com/creating-a-world-of-love-1/

DIVINE DISCUSSIONS, HIGHER REALMS SPEAKING DIRECTLY TO US, Phillip Elton Collins https://phillipeltoncollins.com/books/divine-discussions-higher-realms-speaking-directly-to-us/

GOD'S GLOSSARY: A DIVINE DICTIONARY, by Phillip Elton Collins https://phillipeltoncollins.com/gods-glossary-a-divine-dictionary/

HAPPINESS HANDBOOK, BEING PRESENT IS THE PRESENT, by Phillip Elton Collins https://phillipeltoncollins.com/happiness-handbook-being-present-is-the-present/

JOURNEY OF THE AWAKENED HEART, DISCOVERING YOUR PASSION & PURPOSE, by Jeff Fasano http://theangel-newsnetwork.com/journey-of-the-awakened-heart/

LIFE MASTERY: A GUIDE TO CREATE THE LIFE YOU WANT & THE COURAGE TO LIVE IT, by Joel D. Anastasi. http://theangelnewsnetwork.com/life-mastery/

MANIFESTING MEANINGFUL MOMENTS, selected writings by Phillip Elton Collins https://phillipeltoncollins.com/books/manifesting-meaningful-moments/

MAN POWER GOD POWER, By Phillip Elton Collins https://phillipeltoncollins.com/man-power-god-power/

SACRED POETRY & MYSTICAL MESSAGES, by Phillip Elton Collins https://phillipeltoncollins.com/books/sacred-poetry-mystical-messages/

ST. GERMAIN'S SEVEN ASCENSION DISCOURSES & GLOSSARY, by St. Germain, Part III. https://phillipeltoncollins.com/books/saint-germain-s-seven-ascension-discourses/

THE ASCENSION HANDBOOK, BY THE TWO MARYS, by Joel D. Anastasi http://theangelnewsnetwork.com/the-ascension-handbook/

THE SECOND COMING, by Joel D. Anastasi. http://theangel-newsnetwork.com/the-second-coming/

WEB SITES:

theangelnewsnetwork.com
gabrielsecondcoming.com (Joel D. Anastasi)
journeyoftheawakenedheart.com (Jeff Fasano)
phillipeltoncollins.com